*About this Boo*

In his book *Banana Wars – The Price of Free Trade*, Gordon Myers, a veteran of these wars, provides a splendid review of the journey the banana industry of the Caribbean has travelled in the international marketplace. He traces the story from the late-nineteenth-century beginnings through the era of 'market protection' to the current challenges of an increasingly liberalised trading regime and a complex market condition.
Gordon Myers has written with clarity, sensitivity, and wisdom, a story of life and production for the people of the Caribbean who have been engaged in the banana business for over one hundred years. His is a remarkable book.

*Dr the Hon. Ralph E. Gonsalves*
*Prime Minister of St Vincent and the Grenadines*

Bananas are taken for granted today as part of the diet of ordinary people in industrial countries. In the Windward Islands of the Caribbean, bananas provided around one-third of all jobs and half their export earnings – until recent WTO rulings began to undermine the industry. Much of this trade and employment has now disappeared as a result of these rulings; and at the end of 2005, the EU is due to give up the last non-tariff measures designed to enable this trade to continue. Unemployment, poverty, and further emigration therefore loom over these islanders, or the tempting alternative of growing and trading in illegal drugs. And all because WTO rules take too little account of the problems of tiny island economies and the human cost of rigid application of global free-trade rules.

In this absorbing history, Gordon Myers tells the extraordinary story of how the US government, in response to grievances of one American corporation, led the World Trade Organisation to nullify a European Community commitment to protect the livelihood of small Caribbean banana growers. The WTO's own working practices also emerge as inflexible and myopic.

The story illustrates the inadequacy of an international trading system dominated by free-trade ideology but lacking the flexibility necessary to enable very small and highly vulnerable states, like the Windward Islands, to receive the protection that they need in order to survive. Moreover, increasingly powerful supermarket chains are able to exploit this free-trade framework to insist on ever lower prices, to the short-term benefit of consumers but the serious detriment of growers in the developing world.

This book is a call for new arrangements in the EU that will enable the Caribbean banana industry to survive beyond 2005, and for an outlook in the WTO that gives greater consideration to the needs of very small states with vulnerable economies.

*Banana Wars: The Price of Free Trade*

A Caribbean Perspective

GORDON MYERS

ZED BOOKS
*London & New York*

*Banana Wars: The Price of Free Trade* was first published in 2004 by
Zed Books Ltd, 7 Cynthia Street, London N1 9JF, UK,
and Room 400, 175 Fifth Avenue, New York, NY 10010, USA

www.zedbooks.co.uk

Designed and typeset in Monotype Baskerville by Illuminati, Grosmont
Cover designed by Andrew Corbett
Printed and bound by Biddles Ltd, King's Lynn

Distributed in the USA exclusively by Palgrave Macmillan, a division of
St Martin's Press, LLC, 175 Fifth Avenue, New York, NY 10010

A catalogue record for this book is available from the British Library

Library of Congress Cataloging-in-Publication Data available

ISBN 1 84277 452 2 (Hb)
ISBN 1 84277 453 0 (Pb)

# Contents

List of Figures and Tables     *vii*

Preface     *viii*

Foreword *by Ralph E. Gonsalves*     *x*

1   Introduction     *1*

2   The Beginnings     *5*

3   A Benevolent Empire     *11*

4   The Windward Islands     *18*

5   Banana Wars in the Commonwealth     *22*

6   Judicial Review and Resolve to Reform     *30*

7   The European Community: Pre-1993     *37*

8   The Market and the Major Players     *42*

9   Negotiating the New Regime     *52*

10   The First GATT Challenges, 1993–94     *65*

11  The Birth of the WTO: Compromise at Marrakesh     70

12  Chiquita and the US Campaign     75

13  The First WTO Case     83

14  A Disputed Conformity     91

15  Spin and Reality     101

16  Seeking an Agreed Solution     111

17  Cotonou Complications     120

18  Winners and Losers     125

19  A Threatened Future     137

20  Prospects for Survival     146

21  - Equitable Trading?     154

22  Reflections on the WTO     159

23  Post-mortem     167

Afterword *by Edison James*     171

Appendix: A Climate of Uncertainty     173

Notes     177

Index     185

# List of Figures and Tables

Figure 8.1    Wages of banana workers    *47*

Figure 8.2    EU suppliers, 1990 and 1992    *51*

Table 11.1    Quotas: BFA allocation and actual share    *72*

Figure 16.1    Striking price auctioning system    *113*

Figure 18.1    Retail prices    *126*

Figure 18.2    UK retail banana prices    *127*

Figure 18.3    Windward Islands exports    *130*

Figure 18.4    Windward Islands exports, real value in local currency    *131*

Figure 18.5    EU imports    *135*

Figure 18.6    Ecuador exports    *136*

Figure 21.1    Supermarket Fair Trade banana sales in the UK    *156*

# Preface

This brief study was inspired by my intermittent involvement over many years in the long-running saga of the Caribbean banana trade. In the early 1970s and again in the early 1980s, I was involved as a government official in the now defunct Ministry of Agriculture, Fisheries and Food (MAFF), which was then the lead department on banana trade issues. In the past decade my involvement has been more continuous and direct, through working with the Caribbean Banana Exporters Association (CBEA). So the perspective is inevitably Caribbean. But the aim is to describe as objectively as possible, with the benefit of that experience, the origins and causes of the dispute, the reasons for its outcome, which has proved so damaging to the Caribbean, and possible ways forward.

I am deeply indebted to former MAFF colleagues, who played a key role in the negotiation and administration of the EU banana regimes, for helpful insights and background. I am even more indebted to CBEA colleagues for their generous help and advice, particularly to Bernard Cornibert, Managing Director of Wibdeco, the Windward Islands Banana Development and Export Company; and to John Ellis, CBE, Chairman of Fyffes Group Ltd. Both showed inexhaustible patience in furnishing information and advice. But I alone am responsible for any errors of judgement or of fact.

I also received much help from H.E. Edwin Laurent, until recently Ambassador of the Eastern Caribbean States to the European Community, a role in which he sought for nine years to defend Caribbean trade interests in the EU. Others who kindly advised include Charles Vanoulst, former Chairman of Wibdeco; Chris Parlin, formerly attorney with the Office of the United States Trade Representative, who for a period acted as Counsel to the Caribbean states; Kathy Anne Brown, international trade lawyer and consultant and David Jessop of the Caribbean Council for Europe.

# Foreword
## by Ralph E. Gonsalves

Banana exports have long been crucial to the economic and social life of the Windward Islands. The Islands have already suffered serious economic and social loss as a result of the banana wars and the settlement that was intended to end them. So have Jamaica and Surinam. But the danger is far from over. As I write this, the first shots are being fired in a final battle that will, to a large extent, determine whether the Caribbean banana trade will survive, thrive or die.

The European Union (EU) and the USA struck a deal in April 2001 to bring the banana dispute to an end. The final step in that settlement, on which the Caribbean was not consulted, entails dismantling, by the end of 2005 at the latest, the current quota type arrangements designed to enable the Caribbean to maintain their banana exports to the EU. In their place there will be just a single tariff on other third country imports, from which the Caribbean and other African, Caribbean and Pacific (ACP) countries would be exempt. The crucial issue is the level of that tariff. It must be sufficient to enable the Caribbean trade to continue. Otherwise there will be further unemployment and increased poverty in the Caribbean. The victims are likely to have few viable options to earn a decent, legitimate alternative livelihood. Unfortunately, a campaign has already been launched for a low-level tariff that would have just that effect.

This battle is not just about bananas. It is about the readiness of the WTO and the international trading community to meet the special problems of small island states which have vulnerable economies and very limited natural resources. Without special help, their economies will inevitably be destroyed by the juggernaut of free trade. The principle of special, differential treatment for such cases is beginning to be accepted. The problem is securing it in practice.

The European Union has set a commendable example in its relationship with developing countries and notably in the successive Lomé Conventions that applied from 1975 to 2000. These sought to develop and foster trade, taking account of the special problems of such small vulnerable economies. The new Partnership Agreement of Cotonou, which succeeded Lomé, includes a continued commitment on bananas. This places a moral and legal obligation on the Community to maintain access for the Caribbean on viable terms. It is vital that this is fully honoured in the transition to the new regime due to apply on or before 1 January 2006. This is a major moral challenge to the enlarged Community of twenty-five nations. We hope and pray that they will meet it.

*Dr the Hon. Ralph E. Gonsalves*
*Prime Minister of St Vincent and the Grenadines*

# I

# *Introduction*

This brief study is about the eight-year stand-off between the European Union (EU) and the USA over bananas and its consequences, in particular for small Caribbean states. But the repercussions of the dispute will be felt far beyond the banana trade. The rulings that the World Trade Organisation (WTO) made against preferential terms of access on bananas constitute precedents that will affect other commodities and other developing countries. There are other very small states besides the four Windward Islands that have highly vulnerable economies and that both need and merit protection from the bracing winds of liberalisation and free trade, unleashed with even-handed rigour by the WTO. The banana war was but a symbol of a more universal problem that remains to be resolved.

The dispute was anything but a routine item in a series of trade disputes between the two major trading blocs. It affected many other countries. Those with most at stake, on both sides of the argument, were all developing countries. These included the vulnerable banana growers in Africa and in the Caribbean, whose trade was at issue in the dispute, since their exports depended upon highly preferential terms of access that the EU granted to them under long-standing agreements. On the other side, the USA, which controlled much of the Latin American banana trade, was supported by banana-exporting states of Latin America in attacking these preferential arrangements on the grounds that they unfairly and illegally inhibited their own sales.

The dispute was also noteworthy in demonstrating the power of a single major corporation in the USA profoundly to influence government policy on an international trade issue, without the support or agreement of its US competitors.

In the Caribbean, bananas are grown on very small family farms, often on difficult terrain and in relatively small quantities. Caribbean growers had no hope of competing on price with the vast, industrialised, and much more productive plantations of Latin America. Only the privileged access granted by the EU enabled their banana industries to survive. Yet their economies were very heavily dependent on their banana exports. On three of the four Windward Islands in the Caribbean (Dominica, St Lucia and St Vincent and the Grenadines) bananas provided between 50 per cent and 70 per cent of all export earnings and well over one-third of employment.

The Caribbean was a focal factor in the dispute. Commonwealth Caribbean countries accounted for only a very small fraction of world exports – about 4 per cent in 1990 and 2 per cent in 2000. But the political and economic importance of this trade has been out of all proportion to its size. This is because their economic and social dependence on banana exports was not disputed; nor was the dependence of those exports on special measures of support. This presented the acid test of the compatibility of free-trade rules of the WTO with the economic well-being of small states highly dependent on one product. The results of that test were ominous – and not just for Caribbean banana growers.

The dispute established beyond a doubt that the preferences granted by the EU were not compatible with the rules and philosophy of the WTO. This study looks at the reasons why the WTO found against the EU in these rulings. The consequences of those WTO rulings have already proved severe for the Caribbean and are likely to become much harsher. There are also implications for the future for other commodities, for other states with small vulnerable economies and for the WTO itself.

The UK played a key role in this battle. It accepted a moral and political commitment to the Commonwealth Caribbean because it had fostered the development of the banana industries there. It also, coincidentally, held the presidency of the European Union at the time that the regime was negotiated and played a decisive part in securing its adoption. From beginning to the end of the dispute, the UK was the one steadfast champion of Caribbean interests in the EU.

Throughout the past century, and particularly since the Second World War, the UK has played a crucial role in nurturing and safeguarding the banana industries of these former colonies. This policy has led to the paradox that a country which normally favours trade liberalisation has insisted on a highly protectionist regime for bananas in order to protect vulnerable Caribbean growers.

This was not a policy based on narrow national economic interest. It is true that, for a period following the Second World War, the development of sterling sources of supply was a mutually beneficial measure in response to Britain's shortage of dollars. But these measures continued long after the currency crisis had passed. The outstanding example, much envied by Caribbean banana growers, was the Commonwealth Sugar Agreement that guaranteed a market for specified volumes at negotiated prices. Indeed, the UK even restricted output of UK sugar beet in order to safeguard the market for Commonwealth sugar, albeit to the benefit also of the British companies that refined it. The government of the day likewise fought a tough battle in the Community to ensure preferential access for Caribbean rum as well as Commonwealth sugar and bananas.

In recent decades the British national interest would have been best served by free trade in bananas, a product that Britain consumes but cannot produce. Indeed, Britain's stand on bananas has entailed penalties not only for British consumers but also, at times, for British manufacturers whose exports have suffered discrimination as a retaliatory measure by countries adversely affected by it. This has been accepted as the price of meeting historical and moral obligations to current or former colonial territories – a welcome contrast to the economic exploitation of colonies of previous centuries, notably through the old Navigation Acts.

For bananas this new approach began in the Caribbean at the very beginning of the twentieth century. The early chapters of this book describe the development of the Commonwealth Caribbean industry and the intermittent but crucial role that the imperial government played in this, leading to increasing, tacit acceptance of some moral responsibility for its welfare long after the exporting countries had achieved independence. This responsibility increased, rather than diminished, with UK accession to the European Economic Community (as it then was) in 1973. The UK was thus impelled into a leading role in creating and supporting the fateful single-market regime adopted in 1993, which sparked off the dispute.

The battle was essentially concluded in 2001 with an agreement finally hammered out bilaterally between the two great trading blocs, the EU and the USA, that effectively signalled the end of the Community's efforts to safeguard African, Caribbean and Pacific (ACP) industries. There still remain crucial decisions to be taken before the end of 2005, on the degree of tariff preference to be accorded to the Africans and Caribbeans from 2006 and on any other measures to be taken to help the most vulnerable. Those decisions will determine whether the struggling Caribbean banana industry has any future beyond 2005.

But there is another dimension that will equally influence their fate and that of other growers in developing countries – the supermarkets that now dominate the retail markets. Their competition with each other for market share has led to ever-increasing downward pressure on prices to producers. It is this pressure which makes unqualified trade liberalisation such a threat to the living standards even of the lowest-cost producers.

# 2

# The Beginnings

## The Canary Islands

The banana is an ancient fruit, which evolved in Asia thousands of years ago and spread to other tropical areas. Because it is delicate and highly perishable, it did not come to Britain on a commercial scale until the invention of the steamship in the nineteenth century. Before that, bananas were known in Britain only as a rare and expensive luxury, available to a privileged few when some enterprising sailor brought in a few bunches.[1]

The first significant commercial imports came to Britain in the 1880s from the Canary Islands, which had been growing bananas since at least the fifteenth century, and were only six days away by steamship. From 1884, Elder, Dempster & Co., a major British shipping company with substantial interests in West Africa, started to develop a regular trade in bananas from the Canaries into Liverpool. Then in 1888 a tea importer, Edward Wathen Fyffe, started shipping bananas from the Canary Islands into London, in partnership with a distributor, James Hudson. But Edward Fyffe did not stay the course for long. Elder, Dempster started competing with him in the capital and then his own suppliers in the Canary Islands decided to take over his firm. Edward Fyffe, who had pioneered the London trade, vanished into early retirement. But the firm of Fyffe Hudson lived on.

The Canary Islands' virtual monopoly of the British market was brought to an end in 1901, after the British government took a fateful initiative that transformed the trade. Joseph Chamberlain, the Secretary of State for the Colonies, decided to help Jamaica, then still a British colony, to develop an outlet for their bananas in the UK.

## Jamaica: The US Market

Jamaica's natural market was the United States, which was close enough for bananas to be shipped in sailing vessels. An enterprising sea captain, one George Busch, pioneered shipments to Boston around 1866 and encouraged many small farmers to plant bananas for export. Other entrepreneurs followed this lead, and in 1885 a number of them merged to create the Boston Fruit Company. The trade flourished and by 1899 sales of Jamaican bananas to the USA accounted for 35 per cent of Jamaica's export earnings. Bananas had become a vital part of the Jamaican economy.

From the 1870s, other pioneers had been developing an export trade in bananas from Central America into Southern US ports. The most prominent was a railroad builder in Costa Rica, Minor Keith, who shipped bananas from Central America to New Orleans. Keith had the lion's share of the US market but in 1899 ran into financial difficulties. This led to a merger between Keith, the Boston Fruit Company and a number of smaller enterprises to form the United Fruit Company. The two principal companies had not been in direct competition, since one supplied the Southern USA from Central America and the other the Northeastern US states from the Caribbean, but the rationale of merger was to reduce risks by spreading the sources of supply. This insured against the costly disaster of ships having no freight to carry. The new company had plantations in Jamaica, Panama, Costa Rica, Colombia, Honduras and Santo Domingo, so that when hurricanes or other climatic disasters struck one source, they could always fall back on another. It was to become the world's dominant banana trader, which would in 1986 be reincarnated as Chiquita.

In the 1890s, Jamaica became prey to fears that United Fruit would replace them with alternative sources of supply. Over the decades this would become a recurrent theme. On this occasion the fears were fuelled by reports that United Fruit were developing plantations in Cuba, which was closer to the US market. This perceived threat led the Roman Catholic Bishop of Jamaica,

Bishop Gordon, to travel to England in 1898 to appeal to Joseph Chamberlain to help Jamaica to develop an alternative outlet for their bananas in the UK. In the event, the bishop's fears proved baseless, but his bold suggestion fell on fertile ground.

## An Imperial Enterprise

The bishop's plea fitted well with Chamberlain's ambition to bind the Empire together by strengthening its economic links. Indeed, he would eventually resign from the government in order to be free to campaign (unsuccessfully) for Britain to abandon free trade in favour of tariffs and imperial preference. The bishop could not have found a more sympathetic audience. Developing a market in the mother country for Jamaican bananas was very much in line with his philosophy. It would both help the colony's export trade and facilitate exports of British goods to Jamaica on the westbound voyage.

But the idea was easier to embrace than to carry out. At least one commercial company[2] had already tried and failed to establish a viable trade shipping bananas from Jamaica to England. Chamberlain had to find someone able and willing to take on the commercial risk.

Chamberlain first turned for help to Alfred Jones, chairman of Elder Dempster, who had pioneered the trade from the Canaries, offering him a government subsidy of £20,000 a year, equivalent to around £1 million a year today,[3] for a regular fortnightly service shipping bananas from Jamaica. Jones sent a close aide, Arthur J. Stockley, to Jamaica to examine the prospects. Stockley's report was far from encouraging. Bringing a delicate and highly perishable product 3,000 miles was in itself a gamble. The shipping time was much greater than from the Canaries and the climate much hotter, so that some cooling system would be needed, but techniques for controlling temperatures in ships' holds were still in an experimental phase. Special provision would also be required for transporting, ripening and distributing the fruit once it was unloaded. Moreover, Jamaican bananas were larger than those from the Canaries and from a different plant variety, and no one could predict how traders and consumer would react to them. The project entailed an enormous commercial risk. Jones turned it down.

Another trader then contracted to provide the service, with the subsidy that Chamberlain had proffered, but he failed even to raise the finance for the necessary ships. Chamberlain then set about twisting Jones's arm with an appeal to his patriotism and hints of a knighthood. According to Stockley 'Chamberlain had evidently worked him up to a great pitch of excitement, and I could see that he was determined to act as a saviour and take on the contract.'[4] He did.

Jones agreed to a ten-year contract to provide a fortnightly shipping service for bananas from Jamaica in return for an annual subsidy of £40,000 (about £2 million in current terms). Jones had pressed for £60,000. Half the subsidy was to be met by the colony. Thus began the British government's long involvement with the Caribbean banana trade, which would continue for more than a century, long after Jamaica and other beneficiaries had become independent states.

To develop the trade a new company, Elders & Fyffes Ltd, was created, bringing together the two firms competing in the trade in Canaries bananas. From the outset Stockley, now fully committed, was the brains and driving force of the enterprise. But his original worries proved well founded; the new enterprise encountered a series of costly problems. The existing fruit trade was not equipped, technically or psychologically, to handle Jamaican bananas. So the new company had to set up its own marketing chain in the UK. This entailed buying premises for use as ripening rooms, where the green bananas could be ripened under carefully controlled conditions; it also entailed acquiring additional ships, since a fortnightly service proved insufficient to ensure the commercially necessary continuity of supplies. As a result the new company soon faced bankruptcy.

It was rescued in 1902 by United Fruit, who purchased 45 per cent of Elders & Fyffes' share capital and also guaranteed banana supplies for Fyffes' ships in Jamaica. The alliance with United Fruit gave Elders & Fyffes access to alternative supplies in Latin America when hurricanes or other natural disasters created shortages in Jamaica. In the event, the deal came just in time. The following year, the terrible hurricane of 1903 flattened almost every banana plant in Jamaica. Without the bananas United Fruit provided from other sources, Elders & Fyffes would have gone out of business.

Eleven years later, Elders & Fyffes became a wholly-owned subsidiary of United Fruit, but on the understanding that it was to be left to run its UK business independently. In his autobiography, written twenty-four years later, Arthur Stockley, who negotiated the deal, claimed that this understanding 'has been faithfully carried out'.[5] This was doubtless so for everyday management of the business, but major investment decisions may well have required the approval of United Fruit. It is difficult to conceive of such autonomy in a later age of rapid communications and travel and multinational corporations running global strategies.

By the time that the ten-year subsidy contract expired in 1910, the trade from Jamaica had become firmly established and there was no need for its renewal. But Elder, Dempster & Co, which undertook the original contract with the government to provide a fortnightly shipping service, lost out badly on it. Arthur Stockley claimed that over the ten years of the contract, Jones lost over £400,000 (equivalent to £2 million today) on providing the shipping service, in spite of the annual subsidy of that amount.[6] One contributory factor was that the contract obliged Elder, Dempster to provide the shipping service, even when there were no bananas to carry. But it proved a good deal both for Jamaica and for Elders & Fyffes, which had built up and developed the trade in partnership with United Fruit. Jones received his knighthood in 1901.

The deal had also brought real benefits to British consumers. By 1905 the banana had become the most popular fruit, vying for first place with apples and oranges. It had the great attraction of being both nutritious and cheap. In spite of the long distance travelled and the careful handling required, bananas retailed at one (old) penny a finger. In those days before decimalisation, the pound was made up of 12 shillings (s) each of 12 pence (d), making 240 pence in all, and each penny was made up of four farthings. One penny was equivalent to perhaps 20 pence today.

Yet the end of the subsidy did not prove to be the end of British government involvement in the fortunes of the Jamaican banana trade. In the following decades, emerging policy on Empire trade combined with a series of crises in Jamaica and other West Indies colonies increasingly to entangle the government at Westminster in the affairs of the industry.

# 3

## *A Benevolent Empire*

It has often been the way that measures to help developing colonies happily coincided with the interests of the imperial government. This seemed very much the case during the next phase of development of the Caribbean banana industry.

In 1926 an Imperial Economic Committee had been examining ways of improving the marketing of Empire fruit 'with a view to increasing the consumption of such products in the United Kingdom in preference to imports from foreign countries'.[1] This aim was entirely in the spirit of Joseph Chamberlain's initiative of 1900, but it also reflected the much harsher economic climate that obtained following the First World War. The Committee was keen to secure the economic and social benefits that would accrue to the colonies by selling more produce to the United Kingdom, but they were also explicitly concerned to reduce expenditure of dollars. Britain had emerged from the war with a huge debt to the USA. Repayments of capital and interest were costing US$35 million a year, which made it difficult to maintain the sterling rate against the dollar. Imports of fruit from the USA and other dollar countries added another US$11 million to this burden. Replacing some of this fruit with supplies from the sterling area would therefore help to sustain sterling.

The Committee was also concerned at the potentially adverse effect on both Jamaican producers and UK consumers of the effective monopoly of the United Fruit Company over Jamaican banana exports to Britain through its subsidiary. The Committee suspected that United Fruit were deliberately limiting exports to Britain in order to maintain a desired price level. In any event, they disliked the fact that

British [colonial] supplies are sent largely to foreign markets and, so far
as they are consigned to the United Kingdom, are subject to foreign
control. On the other hand the United Kingdom market is almost
entirely dependent on foreign supplies, over 84 per cent at present
being obtained from the Canaries and from Central America.[2]

All this drove the Committee to recommend exploring ways
to increase supplies from the colonies, including the possibility of
developing exports to the UK from the Windward Islands. The
Committee also supported the ambition of many Jamaicans to
have a new shipping line under British control, but the Committee
insisted that this could only be viable if it were not dependent
on Jamaican supplies alone. The Committee also recommended
government aid for setting up producer organisations, so that there
would be a responsible body with whom shipping companies could
negotiate and which could guarantee fulfilment of contracts.


## Jamaican Growers versus United Fruit

The Committee's report reflected genuine concern among growers
at being totally dependent on the United Fruit Company for access
to the British market. In the light of the Committee's recommendations, the growers were able to set up a co-operative, the
Jamaica Banana Producers Association, with support and financial
aid from the colonial government. This Association not only produced bananas but also established its own shipping service and
its own marketing arrangements in the UK. The object was not
merely to break the United Fruit monopoly as the sole supplier
of Jamaican bananas to the UK, but to establish for themselves
a benchmark by which to determine what was a fair price for
that market.

It took nearly three years and a grant of £1,200 a year to
establish the producer association and to get the banana enterprise off the ground. A key problem was to secure financing for
purchase of ships, for which the colonial government agreed to
guarantee a loan. £1.2 million was initially sought (around £36
million in current terms), but in the event only £200,000 was
needed as a result of a partnership struck with a US shipper. But,

notwithstanding the strong advice of the Economic Committee, the shipping was not shared with any other source of supply.

The co-operative was backed by statute, the Jamaican Co-operative Marketing Association Law, 1928, and members were required to sell 75 per cent of their production from contracted land to the Association. The obligation remained with the land even if it were sold. A statutory levy of one penny per count bunch (comprising nine hands of bananas) was imposed on all banana exports to create a fund to meet any claims arising out of the government loan guarantee.

Through its direct experience of the market and by the competition it provided, the Association was able to raise prices not only for its own 7,700 grower members, who accounted for about a third of Jamaica's total production, but also for those growers contracted to United Fruit. But a few years later, the Association had to appeal for help to the imperial government at Westminster, in the face of a perceived threat to its survival.

The Association claimed that United Fruit had always been opposed to the co-operative. Arthur Stockley had publicly poured scorn on the idea of the subsidised shipping line, when this was first mooted, claiming that it would be 'A complete Fiasco and Hopeless.'[3] The company is said to have threatened never to buy fruit from any grower who signed up to the Association contract.[4] By 1935 the Association was convinced that United Fruit was seeking to destroy it, luring away contracted supplies by paying growers more than the overseas market would bear or the Association could afford.[5] The crisis followed two successive years of hurricanes in 1932 and 1933, which severely reduced supplies available for export. It hardly seems surprising that the shortage should have forced up prices, whatever the motives of United Fruit may have been. Nevertheless, a petition was despatched to the Secretary of State for the Colonies seeking help. The Secretary of State appointed a three-man commission to look into the state of the industry and to make recommendations.

The good offices of the commission helped achieve a satisfactory settlement in 1936, in the form of a Tripartite agreement which also included Standard Fruit, another US company now established as a third buyer on the island. All three agreed to

pay the same price to growers each week, based on a formula
that would reflect movements in prices in the UK, a basis which
earned very satisfactory returns for the growers.[6] Moreover, United
Fruit undertook to buy all the Association's excess bananas and
to make up any shortfall in its supplies, including providing them
from other sources in the event of shortages in Jamaica caused
by drought, hurricane or other natural causes. This enabled the
Association to fill its ships to over 90 per cent capacity, thereby
keeping down freight costs.

In addition, United Fruit and Standard Fruit undertook not to
import bananas into the UK from any other source so long as
Jamaica was able to meet market needs. In return, the Association
agreed to limit its exports to the UK alone, instead of to the USA
and Canada also. The one other concession by the Association
was to convert into a joint stock company in deference to United
Fruit's antipathy to the idea of a successful co-operative that might
set an example to growers elsewhere.[7]

The terms agreed by United Fruit were acknowledged in
Jamaica to be 'extraordinarily magnanimous'[8] and led to a pe-
riod of constructive cooperation between the company and the
Association. One factor that may have helped to ensure this was
the introduction of Imperial Preference in 1932, which, accord-
ing to the Royal Commission already cited, 'was accepted by the
United Fruit Company as a sign of the determination of the British
Government to safeguard the interests of colonial producers'.


## Imperial Preference


British-manufactured exports suffered badly as a result of the
world depression, and the UK ran up a worrying trade deficit.
To mitigate the damage, the national government abandoned both
the Gold Standard and Britain's policy of free trade. The government fell back, instead, on a system of protective tariffs combined
with preferential access for colonial and Empire products. This
was the policy that Joseph Chamberlain had advocated without
success thirty years earlier, in very different circumstances. By a
happy coincidence, it was his son, Neville Chamberlain, who, as

Chancellor of the Exchequer, secured the passage of the Import Duties Bill of 1932, which imposed a 10 per cent duty on most imports from non-Commonwealth countries, including bananas. As one biographer of Joseph Chamberlain points out, 'this was no basis for imperial unity – no more than a shelter in an economic blizzard'.[9] But it was nonetheless welcome to Jamaica for that.

Thanks to Commonwealth preference, Jamaican bananas were exempt from this tariff. This gave an immediate and hefty stimulus to Jamaican exports to the UK and also to Canada. In 1934 the UK overtook the USA for the first time as Jamaica's largest customer for bananas; imports from Jamaica peaked at over 260,000 tons before the Second World War and accounted for 87 per cent of the UK market. The trade had come a long way since the 1920s when imports from Jamaica were less than 60,000 tons and under 40 per cent of UK supplies.

Moreover, growers in Jamaica received a much higher price than growers in Latin America. Jamaican growers were guaranteed a minimum price of 2s 3d per stem, with the actual price reflecting returns on the UK market. In 1939 they received 3s 10d per stem of about 50 lb. This compared to 1s 8d in Colombia, Costa Rica and Honduras for stems averaging between 75 and 125 lb.

Then came the Second World War from 1939 to 1945, which badly affected the Jamaican banana industry because the UK banned imports of fresh bananas. In view of the scarcity of shipping, the Ministry of Food decided in November 1940 that it was better to concentrate on importing a single type of fruit. Bananas were not a strong candidate for this privileged position because ships had to travel across the Atlantic in convoy and therefore at the speed of the slowest. This could prove fatal for such a delicate and perishable fruit. The choice therefore fell on oranges. (In a felicitous human touch, the Ministry failed to give timely warning to the Foreign Office, which wrote complaining that 'we were rather painfully surprised to learn from the "Times" of November 27 that no more licences were going to be issued for the importation of bananas into this country.'[10] It was they who had to soothe protesting ambassadors from exporting third countries.)

However, the government did compensate the colonies for the lost trade. Initially, the UK undertook to purchase in Jamaica, at a fixed price, up to 12 million stems a year, subsequently increased to 14.5 million. In the first year, some of this was successfully exported to North America. But soon the shipping space could not be spared for banana exports. So, from the summer of 1942, UK compensation took the form of a lump-sum payment of £800,000 to be spent at local discretion, but primarily to encourage growers to diversify into production of other food for local consumption. At least the help seems to have been appreciated, to judge by the letter of thanks opposite, which the Jamaica Banana Producers Association sent to London.

Britain provided comparable help to Dominica and St Lucia in the Windward Islands, when lack of shipping prevented their exports to Canada, and to neighbouring Caribbean islands; and to the former German colonies of the Cameroons, then a mandated territory, when exports to Britain ceased to be feasible.

As happens in war, British consumers therefore lost out twice over, paying in taxes for the bananas they were unable to eat. It was a long time before bananas reappeared as a normal item of the British diet. To children who grew up in the war, the first arrivals in 1947 seemed 'an object of magical veneration'.[11] Initially they were reserved for children, pregnant mothers and the elderly; and somehow none reached the Scottish island of Skye until 1957.[12]

But the war marked the end of the Jamaican banana industry as a viable business capable of standing unaided on its own feet. Jamaica had laid claim to being the world's largest exporter, until overtaken by Honduras in 1928;[13] and before the war, bananas had accounted for more than half of Jamaican exports by value,[14] thanks partly to the stimulus provided by imperial preference. But during the war, with the loss of its export markets, the industry suffered serious decline; problems of disease increased; later the Latin American industry expanded. It was never to be glorious summer again.

THE JAMAICA BANANA PRODUCERS' ASSOCIATION LIMITED.

64 Harbour Street, Kingston.
28th August 1941.

Hon. Colonial Secretary,
The Secretariat,
Jamaica.

Sir,

　　We have the honour to advise you of the
following Resolution which was unanimously passed at
our Annual General Meeting to-day:-

　　"That the Government of Jamaica be asked to
　　convey to the British Government an expression
　　of deep loyalty and of the grateful thanks of
　　all banana growers in Jamaica for the Imperial
　　Government's purchase of 12 million stems of
　　bananas at a guaranteed price of 3/- per payable
　　which has kept alive the Jamaica banana
　　industry and has prevented the financial
　　collapse of the entire Colony."

　　We would like to add that due reference was
made to the admirable spirit displayed by the
British people which has won the commendation of
all civilised people throughout the world. Comment
was also made on the fact that, notwithstanding
the dangers and difficulties faced by the British
Government and people, it was found possible to think
of this small Colony and to make such generous
provision for its banana industry.

　　Should you think it desirable that the
resolution should be transmitted by cable, we should
be glad to refund the expense.

　　　　I have, etc.,
　　　　THE JAMAICA BANANA PRODUCERS ASSOCIATION LTD.
　　　　　　(Sgd). L. Gibson.
　　　　　　　　Actg. Secretary

# 4

## The Windward Islands

With the end of the war, the scenario changed. The UK began to import bananas again on a small scale from Jamaica and also from the British Cameroons, but with the Ministry of Food as the sole importer. Then, from January 1953, private trading was restored and all restrictions were lifted on imports from the sterling area. Non-sterling sources were limited to a very small quota, because the UK was desperately short of hard currency.

That relaxation of controls brought an important new Commonwealth player into the game: the Windward Islands. These are the four small islands, still colonies at that time, of St Lucia, Dominica, St Vincent & the Grenadines and Grenada. Their joint population totalled only 420,000, of which the largest island, St Lucia, had about 150,000 and the smallest, Dominica, 70,000. These islands had been much fought over between France and England during the eighteenth century and some of them changed hands a number of times. Though England won in the end, French influence remained in the form of the predominantly French local dialect or patois which is commonly used alongside English.

There had been intermittent attempts in the past to establish an export trade from the Windward Islands. In 1933, the Canadian Banana Company, which was controlled by United Fruit, undertook to buy all bananas of exportable quality, and regular shipments were made from Dominica and St Lucia to Montreal. But due to problems of quality and disease, the trade remained limited and was finally ended by wartime shipping problems in 1942.

In 1949 another company, Antilles Products, started exporting Windward Islands bananas to Ireland but soon ran into financial difficulties. At that time also, the Jamaican Banana Producers Association agreed to divert ships to pick up bananas on the way to the UK, but this proved uneconomic because of the shipping delays it entailed. The colonial government appears to have done little to encourage the development of the export industry. In the 1930s they may have been anxious not to risk undermining the established Jamaican trade.[1] Shortly after the war, Whitehall was more concerned that farmers who switched to bananas might find that there was no market for them.[2]

Two related factors changed all that: the removal of restrictions on imports from non-dollar sources from 1953 and the stimulus this gave to a major entrepreneur to develop a banana export trade in the Islands. This entrepreneur was John van Geest, a son of the Dutch founder of Geest Industries Ltd.

John van Geest became the driving force behind the development of the Windward Islands banana export trade. He made this something of a personal crusade. Geest took over Antilles Products and contracted with each of the Windward Islands to purchase the whole of their output of exportable quality, initially for a ten-year period. This was a daunting undertaking. It entailed challenging the dominant position then enjoyed by Fyffes in the UK market, and setting up a parallel network of ripening and distribution facilities.

Geest bought the bananas from growers at local buying stations and undertook all subsequent operations itself or through a subsidiary company, up to the point of sale to the retailer in the UK. This meant that selection and handling was under its own control, in contrast to the position of Fyffes (see Chapter 5). Geest paid a price for the bananas 'designed to pay a reasonable sum to growers at a steady level all through the year'.[3] This was calculated, however, after deduction of all of Geest's costs, and attempts by the growers to verify just what these costs were proved a perennial cause of friction.[4]

Banana production is not seasonal like sugar cane, and thus offered growers the great advantage of a cash crop for sale every week or fortnight all the year round. Production is labour-intensive and thus promotes employment; and the banana plant recovers quite quickly from the ravages of hurricanes and other climatic disasters to which the region is prone. These factors encouraged the eventual participation of about 27,000 small family farms.[5]

This was a particularly propitious time to develop the export industry in the Windward Islands, because the UK virtually guaranteed them a remunerative market by limiting more competitive imports from Latin America to a token annual quota of 4,000 tons. This nurtured the colonial banana industry as well as saving hard currency. From very small beginnings, Windward Island exports to the UK rose to over 100,000 tons in 1963 and eventually reached a peak of 275,000 tonnes in 1992, the final year of the national regime, far outstripping Jamaica.

This trade transformed the economy of the islands. Previously, sugar had been the staple of West Indian economies, but the trade had suffered badly from the development of the European sugar beet industry, which was supported by heavy import duties and export subsidies. In Dominica, other products had formerly flourished. Limes had originally been important, but their export market for natural lime juice had then been destroyed by competition from synthetic substitutes. Limes were then replaced by vanilla, which became the main source of income in the 1940s, but this too was driven out by cheaper products.

Following a number of civil disturbances during the 1930s, the UK had set up a Royal Commission in 1938 to carry out a comprehensive survey of the state and needs of all the British colonies in the West Indies. Its report,[6] completed in 1939, constitutes an implicit indictment of the colonial administration. There were very few roads to serve rural communities, and most were little more than dust tracks; children walked barefoot; dwelling houses were small, often with mud floors and a thatch roof, with none of the conveniences now taken for granted. As the Royal Commission put it, 'Housing is generally deplorable and sanitation primitive in the extreme.' Similarly, the provision of teachers and schools in the Islands was totally inadequate. The report was sufficiently embarrassing for the government to defer publication to avoid giving propaganda material to its enemies during the war, although they had been no more successful in dealing with problems of social deprivation at home. When the report was finally submitted to Parliament in June 1945, the government at the same time announced measures designed to bring about improvements.

The report concluded that 'Of all the British West Indian Islands, Dominica presents the most striking contrast between the great poverty of a large proportion of the population ... and the beauty and fertility of the island.' In the years following the war, Dominica was probably the most deprived of the Windward Islands and St Lucia the least, having benefited from the presence of a US base. But the differences were only of degree.

Bananas transformed life on the islands. Small farmers could obtain forest land for clearing and planting at token prices with interest-free loans. Earnings from bananas enabled children to walk to school in shoes and the primitive huts to be improved. Infrastructure was developed and new schools and hospitals built.

Yet the banana export trade that contributed so much to raising the quality of life in the islands was based on production from small subsistence farms averaging less than one hectare (2.4 acres) in area and often on steep hill land. The small farmers could not afford irrigation, which was in any event not practicable for the majority of farms because of the nature of the terrain. Yield therefore tended to vary according to the rainfall pattern in any year. The Islands are also prone to climatic disasters such as drought and hurricane, which in an average year will result in a loss of about 5 per cent of the crop.

As a result of these factors, the average grower had difficulty achieving a yield of even 16 tons to the hectare, compared to over 50 tons to the hectare produced in Latin America on plantations covering thousands of hectares. With the low yield on a very small area, the Windward Island grower needed a much higher margin to be able to survive. In addition, shipping costs were higher for the Islands, entailing stops at four different ports. The islands therefore had no possibility of competing on price with Latin American production. The industry depended entirely on the protection provided by the restricted UK market. So did that in Jamaica. Although the farming structure in Jamaica was less fragmented, it shared similar problems of size, scale and climate. If this protection were significantly weakened, let alone removed, these industries would collapse.

# 5

## *Banana Wars in the Commonwealth*

### Jamaica

The Jamaican industry had suffered badly in the war from the loss of its markets, as well as from a hurricane in 1944, and the area under bananas was down to one-third of its pre-war level. Once restrictions were lifted post-war, Jamaican exports recovered in the 1950s to around 150,000 tons a year. But because of rising costs of inputs, the industry had difficulty in making ends meet and in 1955 Jamaica asked the UK government to introduce a deficiency payments system for Jamaican bananas, making up the difference between the average market price and a desired base price of £65 10s per ton.

Whitehall reacted unfavourably, the Colonial Office pontificating that 'HMG cannot embark on a general policy of underwriting prices of, or guaranteeing markets for, colonial commodities.'[1] This was certainly not the government's approach on sugar. Because they were particularly concerned to ensure adequate supplies from sterling sources, the UK government negotiated the Commonwealth Sugar Agreement, which did indeed provide a guaranteed market and guaranteed prices for specified volumes of cane sugar from each Commonwealth supplier. Moreover, the government took powers under the Sugar Act of 1956 to restrain domestic UK sugar beet production in order to ensure that the market had room for contracted Commonwealth supplies.

For bananas, the government instead urged Jamaica to set up a price stabilisation fund, which could be used to supplement grower returns in bad times from contributions made when prices were more remunerative. The government offered to lend, interest-free, half the sum required to set this up. This was accepted, although the terms did not go nearly as far as Jamaica considered necessary.[2] A similar facility was also offered to the Windward Islands.

## Increased Protection for the Commonwealth

The government decided also to increase the tariff protection for Commonwealth bananas. The tariff had remained unchanged at £2 10s od per ton since 1932 and its incidence had fallen from 10 per cent to about 4 per cent. In 1947 that rate had been bound in the GATT to Brazil, which had been by far the largest third-country (non-Commonwealth) banana supplier to the UK in the immediate pre-war years. With some difficulty, the government persuaded Brazil in 1956 to agree to a tripling of the duty to £7 10s od per ton (about 12 per cent) in return for the removal of UK import duties on brazil nuts.

Although all restrictions on non-dollar sources were lifted in 1955, this tripling of the duty on non-Commonwealth bananas in the following year made imports from the Canary Islands un-economic. As a result, the UK market was effectively reserved for Jamaica, the British Cameroons and the Windward Islands. Then in 1961 the British Cameroons had to drop out of the market because they lost their Commonwealth status and therefore their duty-free entry. The United Nations' Trustee Committee required them to choose in a referendum between joining with Nigeria or French Cameroun. They opted for French Cameroun and left the Commonwealth. As a result, Jamaica and the Windward Islands enjoyed a virtual monopoly of the UK market.

## The Domestic Banana War

This provoked competition between them for market share, resulting in a so-called 'Banana War', which produced oversupply and low prices and threatened the viability of the industry in both countries. To avert this, Jamaica and the Windward Islands agreed in 1966 to share the market on the basis of 52 per cent for Jamaica and 48 per cent for the Windwards. Vital to this deal was an agreement by Fyffes (the major shipper of Jamaican bananas) and Geest not to bring in bananas from any other source unless Jamaica and the Windward Islands could not between them meet UK needs. Such an arrangement could not be made without the concurrence of the UK government, which acquiesced in the deal subject to the provisos that prices were not maintained 'unreasonably' above comparable free-market prices, that other Commonwealth countries were not excluded, and that the government's position in regard to the Restrictive Trade Practices Act 'was not compromised'.[3] The last seems a curious proviso, since the Act prohibits both market sharing and exclusivity arrangements. In any event, the deal did not work out.

For a variety of reasons, including severe drought in 1967/8, Jamaica was unable to maintain its tonnage, so that Geest constantly increased its market share, a trend that had begun in 1956. This caused particular anguish to Fyffes, which depended on Jamaica for supplies and therefore for profitability. In contrast to the position at the time in the Windward Islands, the Jamaican Banana Board retained ownership of Jamaican bananas right up to the doors of the ripening rooms in the UK. The Board employed Fyffes as its agent to handle 77.5 per cent of its banana exports and Jamaica Producers to handle the remaining 22.5 per cent. Fyffes saw their market share decline from 59 per cent in 1956 to 38 per cent in 1969, while Geest's share rose from 11 per cent to 51 per cent.[4] Fyffes' profits fell from around £1 million a year in the 1950s and early 1960s to their first ever net loss in 1966.[5] Fyffes blamed their woes largely on Jamaican failure to meet past promises on both volume and quality.

Fyffes decided that this could not continue and gave notice of termination of both their Agency agreement and their undertaking not to import from other origins. But they were prepared to continue importing on the basis of volumes and prices agreed week by week.

Jamaica saw this as a plot both to depress prices and to ditch Jamaica in favour of other sources of supply, such as the Ivory Coast, which also benefited from duty-free access following UK accession to the European Community (see Chapter 7). They claimed that Fyffes' parent company, United Fruit, had already destroyed the Dominican Republic's banana-export industry simply by terminating its contract with them and were now poised to give them similar treatment. The Jamaican prime minister appealed to the UK government to help by providing greater protection against imports from non-Caribbean sources.

## The Denning Report

In the event, the government suggested appointing Lord Denning, then Master of the Rolls, as a conciliator between the Jamaica Banana Board and Fyffes, 'with a view to their reaching such agreement ... as takes account of all the interests concerned'. Lord Denning would have preferred to act as arbitrator, but Fyffes could not agree to commit their shareholders to whatever decision emerged. Denning found the role of conciliator as 'almost impossible' and considered his report on bananas the least rewarding task he had undertaken.[6]

In his report, Lord Denning contrasted the Jamaican and Windwards industries:

> The Windwards industry (apart from the setback of the recent hurricane) is healthy and prosperous, showing a good return to the Windwards growers and also to the UK importers. The Jamaican industry is sick and losing money both for Jamaica itself and for the UK importers.[7]

He noted that Fyffes and the Jamaican Banana Board had been on bad terms for many years and blamed the final breakdown in relations partly on the inefficiency of the industry in Jamaica. But he also noted the intentions of a new Banana Board to undertake a radical improvement programme.

Lord Denning suggested a number of possible ways forward but none commanded agreement of all the parties. He sadly concluded:

> Seeing that none of my proposed solutions is acceptable, I can do no more. I must leave it now to the Governments of the UK and

Jamaica to bring peace and stability to the industry, if they can. It is a nigh hopeless task because of the suspicion and distrust which exist on both sides. Yet each side needs the other. If they go on as they are, each will pull the other down. I only hope that good sense will prevail in time to save them.[8]

Happily, it did. But the government was first subjected to powerful appeals jointly from the Jamaican and Windward Island governments for action to prevent Fyffes from supplying the UK increasingly from West African sources, which they feared would result in the collapse of the UK market.

The government was in a dilemma. A new and more enterprising Banana Board in Jamaica had proposed a major restructuring plan, costing £4 million, to improve the efficiency of the industry, but was reluctant to proceed with it without some assurance that Fyffes would not undermine the market. But Jamaican fears of Fyffes' motives were not borne out by Lord Denning, who had pointed out that 'Fyffes have imported a good deal from elsewhere, but in most weeks this has barely sufficed to make up the shortfall' from Jamaica and the Windwards. Moreover, the government could not require a UK company to trade on a basis that was contrary to the interests of its shareholders. They could not therefore impose the mandatory system of arbitration on issues of price or volumes that Jamaica was seeking and Denning had proposed, even had they wanted to do so.

But the government also had no wish to increase the already substantial protection of the market, since this would do nothing to stimulate necessary improvements in the Jamaican industry, and would be contrary to consumer interests and damaging to trading relations with other countries. Ecuador, the leading dollar banana exporter, had already imposed occasional sanctions against certain UK exports in retaliation for the restrictions of the dollar quota. More worrying, the USA had begun complaining about the quota restrictions on dollar imports of bananas and other products (rum, citrus and cigars), which could no longer be justified on currency grounds and the USA considered to be in breach of the GATT.

The furthest the government was prepared to go was to undertake 'to take action to restore stability to the market if prices were seriously undermined as a result of increasing imports of non-Commonwealth bananas'. The compromise eventually reached included a commitment by the Jamaican Banana Board to attempt to increase volumes and maintain quality and an undertaking by Fyffes to import non-Caribbean bananas only to the extent of any shortfall in Caribbean supplies.

The government also sought to improve the system of market regulation by setting up in 1973 a Banana Advisory Committee, chaired by the Ministry of Agriculture, Fisheries and Food (MAFF)[9] and comprising representatives of the three major importers and the Jamaican and Windwards trading bodies (Jamco and Winban). Their role was purely advisory and their main task was to review prospective supplies from different sources on an annual basis, updated monthly, so that decisions on admitting additional supplies from the dollar area could be taken on as well-informed a basis as possible.

Unfortunately, supplies from Jamaica continued to decline and those from the Windward Islands were more variable, due partly to a series of climatic disasters, culminating in hurricanes David in 1979 and Allen in 1980. The combined Jamaica/Windwards share of the UK market fell from 97 per cent in 1969 to 32 per cent in 1980. To make up for the shortfalls from these origins, Fyffes increasingly turned to other sources. In addition to imports from West Africa, Fyffes decided to foster the development of the industry in Belize (former British Honduras) and in the former Dutch colony of Surinam. These developments made a significant contribution to the economies of those two countries. In the case of Belize, the development included creating a new deep-water port to permit direct shipments from the south of the country, with aid from UK and EU agencies and the World Bank.

## Jamaican Problems

Jamaican exports reached a post-war peak of 205,000 tons in 1966. Thereafter, they fell every year bar one to hit 70,000 in 1975 and remained around that level till Hurricane Allen devastated production in August 1980. Notwithstanding the hurricane, this

presents a stark contrast with Jamaica's strong pre-war performance, when it produced up to 360,000 tons for the US, UK and
European markets. Production had collapsed in the past but had
then recovered. In 1917, following hurricanes in three successive
years, exports fell to 32,000 tons, but they were fully restored in
two or three years. Why did this not happen post-war, in spite of
the advantage of a protected market in the UK?

The answer may lie partly in the political and economic problems affecting the Jamaican economy as a whole in much of this
period. The massive increase in oil prices in 1973 had a devastating effect on the economy of Jamaica, as also of the Windward
Islands. The high cost of oil had a knock-on effect on other goods,
created inflationary pressures and led to mounting public debt.
For bananas, the oil price rise increased the cost of inputs such
as fertilisers and above all the cost of shipping. The fall in export
volumes made this particularly painful, since half-empty holds
meant 'shipping air' at high freight costs.

Moreover, these difficulties hit an economy that had already
incurred substantial debts in pursuit of Prime Minister Michael
Manley's radical programme of 'social democracy' and social welfare reform. Matters were made worse by a credit squeeze imposed
by US agencies and commercial banks, which were hostile to that
policy and above all to the personal and political ties that Michael
Manley went out of his way to forge with Cuba.

The consequence for the Jamaican economy was devastating.
Between 1974 and 1980 gross domestic product fell by 16 per cent;
unemployment rose from 24 per cent to 31 per cent and the cost
of living rose by 320 per cent. The exchange rate against the
US dollar fell from J$0.88 to J$1.76. 'For ordinary Jamaicans, the
reforms of the Manley government had produced a severe decline
in living standards, worse unemployment, and a mood of depression that pervaded the whole economy and society.'[10]

This general economic malaise in itself may suffice to explain
the lack of drive and efficiency in the industry in that period. But
developments specific to the banana sector that occurred a good
deal earlier also played their part.

The spread of Panama disease, which attacks the roots of
banana plants, in the 1940s and 1950s had led growers to switch

from the Gros Michel variety to the more resistant Lacatan, but, unfortunately, the skin of the Lacatan banana is more susceptible to scarring. This caused problems because the appearance of the banana skin is perceived as an important quality factor, even though the skin is not eaten.

Then in 1967 Jamaica was required to ship bananas in boxes, instead of on the stem, in line with the practice developing in Latin America, as Chapter 8 describes more fully, but this did not bring the expected improvement in quality of the bananas exported. This was because the fruit tended to incur damage in transit to the ports, since it was still carried manually from the field to the boxing stations and from there taken by lorry to the ports. It was especially vulnerable during loading and unloading. As a result, importers complained that they were obliged to sort and repack all the boxes on arrival, thus adding substantially to costs.

In contrast, the move to boxing in Latin America was seized as an opportunity to raise quality and to promote brand identity linked to quality. A key element was the cleaner, unscarred skin of the Latin American fruit, and the contrast with the appearance of Caribbean bananas became increasingly manifest in the market.

In addition, the high cost of investing in the switch to boxing, including, on the larger farms, installing overhead cableways to carry the fruit, led most of the large growers still in the business to depart. At the same time, shortage of foreign exchange led to shortages of all imported inputs, from fertilisers to spare parts for aircraft needed to spray plants to control leaf spot disease.

By the early 1980s, falling Caribbean volumes combined with continuing poor performance on quality to cause growing dissatisfaction in the UK. Just at that time, in 1983, a disgruntled banana trader threw a political spotlight on to the anomaly of this highly restricted banana market. He sought and obtained a judicial review of the way the system was being administered.

# 6

## Judicial Review and Resolve to Reform

### A Legal Challenge

In November 1982, a banana trader who had applied unsuccessfully for additional import licences for dollar bananas sought and obtained a judicial review of the government's decision by a High Court judge.

Originally, licences for imports of dollar bananas had been awarded to the three companies importing from the Caribbean – Fyffes, Geest and Jamaica Producers – but independent fruit traders were subsequently allocated a share. Chris International Foods was one of twenty-four such companies. It persistently objected to the fact that most of the dollar licences, about 86 per cent, still went to the big three importers. Then in 1978 a change to the system reduced the share of the independents still further. This provoked much fruitless correspondence with the Ministry of Agriculture, Fisheries and Food (MAFF), culminating in the refusal of an application by Chris International for a supplementary licence. Chris International then sought and was granted leave to apply for a judicial review of that refusal.

The role of the Judge, Mr Justice Hodgson, was not to pronounce on the appropriateness of the import policy but on the process by which the decisions on licence allocation were reached. But counsel for Chris International, the applicants, challenged the legality of the whole system of restricting dollar banana imports. The requirement for import licences was imposed by statutory instrument[1] under powers conferred by emergency legislation passed immediately before war was declared in 1939. The applicants argued that the objective of that Act could not include the control of imports of dollar bananas in order to protect the trade of the Commonwealth Caribbean.

Mr Justice Hodgson's reaction was intriguing:

> I do not find this at all an easy matter. At first sight it seems an unlikely situation that perhaps most of the licences regulating imports into this country since the end of the War have been ultra vires because not concordant with the objects and policy of the 1939 Act, but the applicant's argument is a strong one. And it is perhaps no less surprising that, in 1983, the Secretary of State for Trade can, at a stroke of the pen, close the frontiers of the United Kingdom to the import and export of all goods, deriving his authority so to do from an order made in 1954 which was never laid before Parliament, the order itself being made under an Act of Parliament which passed through all its stages in both Houses of Parliament in one day and was expressed to continue in force only until 'such date as His Majesty may by Order in Council declare to be the date on which the emergency that was the occasion of its passing came to an end'.[2]

However, the judge did not find it necessary to decide on that difficult issue because the applicant manifestly succeeded on his second argument. This was that the licensing powers had been granted under this legislation to the Secretary of State for Trade but had been effectively delegated to the Minister of Agriculture, Fisheries and Food. Mr Justice Hodgson agreed that the Secretary of State had no legal right to make this transfer.

Chris International thus won a technical ruling against the way that the system was administered. But the company got no more licences. However, Krishna Maharaj, who ran the company and initiated the action, merits a footnote in history for doing so. Also, regretfully, for the more mournful reason that he has been languishing since 1987 in a Florida jail for a double murder that he adamantly maintains that he never committed. The first ten years he spent on death row until his death sentence was commuted to life imprisonment in 1997. His friends and supporters, including two British Members of Parliament, have long been campaigning for a retrial on the basis of new evidence to support his claim.

Mr Justice Hodgson's ruling necessitated formal changes in the way that the import licensing arrangements were administered in order to give a more direct role to the Department of Trade. More important, however, was its effect in confronting Margaret Thatcher's radical Conservative government with the apparent conflict between the complex regulation of the UK banana market and their zealous campaign to 'set the people free' by deregulation and liberalisation. The judicial review highlighted the fact that the people were far from free when it came to buying bananas. It was the government that decided what volume of bananas it was appropriate for Britons to consume, who should import them and where from; and in doing so, it gave priority to bananas which were generally more expensive and less consistent in quality than those available from alternative sources.

## Policy Review

Since this case followed mounting frustration over poor quality and low volumes from the Caribbean, voices in Whitehall suggested that the time might be ripe to sweep away these controls. The Department of Trade, in particular, was traditionally concerned to promote greater liberalisation and was concerned at the threats and occasional reality of retaliation against UK exports by countries such as Ecuador, which felt aggrieved by the restriction imposed on their banana exports. More significantly, the USA had gone so far as to lodge a formal complaint in the GATT in 1972, claiming that the dollar quotas on bananas and other products were no longer justified on currency grounds and therefore were in breach of the Agreement. Although the USA secured a panel to look into the complaint, the issue was settled bilaterally. But this was an omen of things to come.

Nevertheless, after some heart-searching the government decided that it had to stick to the existing regime, subject, however, to very firm commitment to reform in the Caribbean. The key UK demand was that, in return for its privileged position on the market, Jamaica should meet specific quality standards. Joint machinery was set up to ensure that this was achieved. This took the form of a UK/Jamaica Banana Quality Monitoring Committee, which set quality standards and reviewed performance. This was measured by points awarded following inspection of every consignment on arrival. A similar joint committee was set up with the Windward Islands. This system, together with other measures taken, led to major improvements over time in quality and packaging.

Jamaica also undertook a major restructuring of its banana industry, following the devastation caused by Hurricane Allen. The plan was to concentrate export production on three large farms, diverting other growers to supplying the domestic market. The main farm was to comprise 10,000 acres of potentially good, flat, banana land currently devoted to sugar. The farm would have an up-to-date infrastructure, including irrigation and cableways, with help from the Commonwealth Development Corporation. The balance of its export would be provided from two farms of around 500 acres each, which were substantial by Caribbean standards. Moreover, a contract was signed with United Fruit (at that time known as United Brands) to manage the project as well as invest in it.

In the event, only the first instalment of 1,800 acres was purchased for the main farm, Eastern Estates. The Jamaican government was unable or unwilling to secure transfer of the remaining lands that had been promised. The establishment of the 1,800-acre farm and the two other smaller centres at Victoria and St Mary's, was nevertheless a major step forward; and United Brands (Fyffes' American parent company) was contracted to manage the farm.

In 1985, Jamaica set up the Banana Export Company, BECO, owned by the growers and dependent on earnings from the UK market. This had the effect of bringing home to growers the link between their income and performance, especially on quality.[3]

### The Decisive Factor: A Moral Responsibility

Both morally and politically, the government of the day really had little alternative to maintaining the protective arrangements because the consequences of ending them were too dire to contemplate. Banana exports to the UK had by then become crucial to the Caribbean, above all to the economies of the Windward

Islands. They accounted for about 50 per cent of all export earnings of three of the four islands and gave employment, directly or indirectly, to about one-third of the working population, in a region with 20 per cent unemployment. These small islands were more dependent on their banana exports than any other state in the world.

As Chapter 4 explained, the development of the banana trade to the UK had transformed the life on the islands from the parlous conditions noted by the Royal Commission in 1939. By the 1980s, the economy of the islands had greatly improved, although there was still much unemployment. But bananas *were* the economy – and they depended entirely on the protected UK market. It was impossible to contemplate pulling the plug on these island economies and plunging them back into their former poverty.

In other Caribbean states, bananas were less crucial to the economy as a whole than in the Windward Islands. In Jamaica they accounted for little over 4 per cent of total export earnings in 1991, but production was concentrated in the three counties of Portland, St Mary and St Thomas, and loss of the trade would cause severe unemployment and economic hardship to those areas. The situation was similar in Belize and Surinam.

The problem was – and remains to this day – that Caribbean banana production simply cannot compete on price with bananas from Latin America. Production, particularly in the Windward Islands, tends to be on small farms and largely on hilly land. The crop has to rely essentially on rain, since irrigation for the small farms would be very expensive and is in many places impracticable. But reliance on rain alone leads to large variations in yield. Shipping costs in the Caribbean are also high because vessels have to load at several ports, and because the variable volumes available increase unit costs.

This contrasts with the vast flat plantations in Latin America, often many thousands of hectares in size, which are operated on an industrial basis, with huge investments in mechanisation and irrigation. Soil depths and mineral contents are better in Latin America and provide a yield per hectare more than double that in the Caribbean. Moreover, large areas of plantation land are situated around ports dedicated to banana shipments. These factors offer substantial economies of scale. As a result, export prices for Latin American bananas were less than half the level in the Caribbean.

If the UK were to remove the protection under which the Caribbean industry had been encouraged to develop, the industry would be destroyed. This would create economic and social turmoil to a degree that would be politically unthinkable. As Dame Eugenia Charles, the charismatic prime minister of Dominica, subsequently put it: 'If we lost the industry completely, we would lose the country. It would be the beginning of despair.'[4] That is why the UK stuck to its policy of protection, insisting only, in return, on measures to ensure satisfactory quality for the British consumer.

Moreover, the consequences of a collapse of the Caribbean banana industry would not be confined to the few exporting countries. The damage could be far more widespread, because of the potentially adverse impact on the common Eastern Caribbean currency, which had remained stable at EC$2.7 to US$1 since 1971; and because of the close trading relationships between members of the Caribbean Economic Community (CARICOM). Loss of banana income would reduce the ability of the exporting states to maintain imports from their trading partners.[5]

These concerns have motivated UK policy to the present day. In bananas, an ethical trade policy has consistently been given priority over free trade. John Selwyn Gummer, as Minister of Agriculture, stressed the moral dimension of this policy in response to questions by the House of Commons Agriculture Committee in December 1992 about ongoing negotiations for the common market regime for bananas:

> I am absolutely committed to the protection of the ACP producers. I think we have not only a legal responsibility but a fundamental moral responsibility. These are societies which depend upon bananas to a degree which is incomprehensible unless you have actually studied the matter. Secondly they are societies which are stable and democratic. They have governments which have sought to carry forward policies which most of us would see as remarkably progressive in the circumstances in which they find themselves. Put that together and you do have moral responsibility which goes beyond the legal responsibility, which itself is very clear and onerous.[6]

The moral responsibility dated back a long way. The legal responsibility arose from the UK accession to the European Community on 1 January 1973. The development of UK policy on bananas must now be seen in this wider European context.

# 7

## *The European Community: Pre-1993*

### UK Accession

The UK had stood aside from the original moves to create the European Economic Community. At that time, in the 1950s, Britain favoured a simple free-trade area and was reluctant to get involved in the more integrated partnership envisaged by the six founding members: France, Germany, Belgium, the Netherlands, Italy and Luxembourg. These signed the Treaty of Rome in 1958, after three years of negotiations. A subsequent British application to join was vetoed by General de Gaulle in January 1963, against the wishes of the five other members, but the UK was finally admitted on 1 January 1973, together with Denmark and the Irish Republic. Spain, Portugal and Greece followed in 1986.

When the UK acceded, the Community was still primarily a customs union, apart from a common and complex system of agricultural support, financed by common funds and swallowing over three-quarters of the Community budget. But there was from the outset a commitment to create a closer union. In October 1972, heads of government (including Edward Heath for the UK) had agreed to the objective of progressive movement towards Economic and Monetary Union. More relevant to the banana saga was the crucial agreement by heads of government, including Margaret Thatcher for the UK, in February 1986, to the Single European Act.

## The Single European Act

This Act provided for a range of measures, including increased powers for the European Parliament, designed to further the process of transforming the European Economic Community into a 'European Union'. The most important was the commitment to establish, by 31 December 1992, an internal market 'without internal frontiers, in which the free movement of goods, persons, services and capital is ensured'.[1] The UK strongly supported the Single European Act in accordance with its wider trade policy, but in the case of bananas this commitment imposed severe problems for the UK and for the Community.

## Bananas in the Community

At the time of UK accession, there was no common regime for bananas; each of the nine member states was free to apply its own import arrangements. The majority – Germany, Belgium, Holland, Luxembourg, Denmark and the Irish Republic – offered unrestricted access for imports. France, Italy and the UK operated restrictive import regimes in order to protect their own banana growers and/or imports from former colonies.

All except Germany applied the common tariff of 20 per cent *ad valorem* to third-country imports. Germany had negotiated a special exemption under a protocol to the Treaty of Rome permitting duty-free imports of the volumes needed for Germany's domestic consumption. This was a curious provision for a common market for which a uniform tariff is the most basic requirement. It was conceded at the eleventh hour at head-of-state level. But insistence on it was symptomatic of German sensitivity at the time to their lack of the strong colonial links such as France enjoyed, since Germany had been deprived of its African colonies in 1919. (The former German East Africa had nevertheless continued supplying bananas to Germany up to the Second World War.)

The Irish Republic, following its accession in 1973, belatedly sought to build on this precedent and put in a bid for duty-free entry or alternatively for a duty-free quota.[2] But it lacked the leverage at the disposal of Chancellor Adenauer in 1958 and the bid never really got off the ground.

Following accession, the UK had to make only two adjustments to its banana import regime in order to conform to Community rules. It had, over the transition period to 1977, progressively to switch from its previous specific tariff of £7.50 per tonne, equivalent to roughly 10 per cent *ad valorem*, to the Community tariff of 20 per cent. It had also to extend the right of duty-free entry to former colonies and associated territories of other member states. The immediate impact of this was to make the UK market more attractive to the Ivory Coast and (French) Cameroon. These were former French colonies, which already enjoyed substantial rights in the French market. Jamaica and the Windward Islands soon regarded them as a potential threat to their position in the UK, as we saw in Chapter 5.

There was one other change we had to get used to: a statistical switch from imperial to metric measurement – from tons to tonnes. The traditional long ton of 2,240 pounds had to yield to the metric tonne of 1,000 kilograms or 2,204.6 pounds for recording banana imports and exports (a change reflected hereafter in this book).

France maintained a highly regulated market for bananas, primarily for the benefit of its own domestic producers. Under the French constitution, the Caribbean islands of Martinique and Guadeloupe, which are close neighbours of the Windward Islands, form part of Metropolitan France and are represented in the French National Assembly. Their bananas are therefore treated as domestic production, not imports. But because they are part of France, they are subject to French social and employment laws, which increase production costs. The French market was therefore regulated to ensure them a remunerative return that took account of these higher costs. To this end, import volumes were limited and two-thirds of permitted imports were reserved for bananas from those overseas departments. The balance was reserved for imports from two former French colonies, the Ivory Coast and Cameroon.

Italy restricted its market to give priority to imports from its former colony in Somalia. This supplied only about 10 per cent of Italy's banana imports. The balance came from Latin America.

When Spain, Portugal and Greece acceded in 1986, all three had restricted markets, for the benefit of domestic producers in the Canary Islands, Madeira and Crete respectively. However, Greece changed its policy and removed all import restrictions in February 1990. The accession of Spain meant that bananas from the Canaries again entered the UK duty-free.

Community growers had even higher production costs than the Commonwealth Caribbean and were therefore even less able to withstand competition from Latin America. This reflected the more difficult terrain and climate in the Canaries and Madeira as well as the imposition of metropolitan wage rates and social legislation in the French Caribbean Islands. The tightly regulated national markets were therefore essential for their viability.

The diversity of national regimes, together with the need to protect the Community's domestic producers, made the creation of a single market regime a formidable task. In addition to these factors, the regime would have to take account of the Community's treaty commitments to certain African and Caribbean states under the Lomé Convention.

## The Lomé Conventions

A key feature of the Community arrangements was a remarkable treaty, the Lomé Convention, between the EU and developing countries in Africa, the Caribbean and the Pacific (consequently referred to as ACP countries). This Convention built on earlier agreements between the original Community of Six and nineteen developing countries with historic links to them. But under those agreements there was a requirement that the developing countries should give reciprocal tariff concessions in return for those provided by the Community. The UK, together with some ACP countries, insisted on dropping that requirement for Lomé.

The Convention was a wide-ranging treaty designed to promote the economic, cultural and social development of these ACP states through comprehensive EU programmes of both trade and aid. It was buttressed by a unique system of joint institutions, comprising a Community–ACP Council of Ministers and a Community–ACP Parliamentary Assembly, through which continuing dialogue and cooperation were pursued.

The first Lomé Convention, signed in 1974, was between the 9 member states that then made up the Community and 45 ACP countries. This operated for five years from 1975. There were three more agreements, the first two for five years and the last for ten, running till the year 2000. This was signed by the 12 states that were then members (increased to 15 in 1995) and 71 ACP countries. The Agreement aimed 'to create a model for relations between developed and developing states'.[3]

The trade provisions included duty-free entry for many agricultural products important to the ACP, improved access for most other agricultural imports, and special protective measures for a few key commodities, such as bananas, sugar and rum.

Each Convention included a specific protocol on bananas. This provided that 'In respect of its banana exports to the Community markets, no ACP state shall be placed, as regards access to its traditional markets and its advantages on those markets, in a less favourable situation than in the past or at present.' The precise purport of this circuitous phraseology would later become the subject of much learned debate by international trade lawyers.

When Lomé IV was being negotiated the Community was already committed to move to a single market. The ACP were naturally anxious about the effect this could have on their banana exports. At their instance, the Convention therefore included an annex that specified that the banana protocol would not prevent the Community from establishing a single import regime 'in full consultation with the ACP', provided that the terms of that protocol were honoured. This was the one assurance on which the Caribbean and other ACP countries had to rely that the single market regime would not remove their protected status and expose them to unfettered competition from Latin America.

Before we can follow the fateful negotiations for the common banana regime, we need to consider the background of the wider world market, which would profoundly affect the nature of any new regime.

# 8

## The Market and the Major Players

### The Global Picture

It is one thing to grow bananas to sell locally; it is quite another to export them to distant markets. That is a much more difficult and risky operation, since bananas are delicate and highly perishable, and only careful handling and treatment will enable them to reach distant markets in good condition. So most bananas are grown to be eaten locally. The world's largest producer, India, exports none. In 1990, less than 20 per cent of world production was exported.

By far the largest exporting region in the world is Latin America, primarily Ecuador, Costa Rica, Colombia, Guatemala, Honduras and Panama. At the time that the European regime was negotiated, Latin American countries together accounted for over 80 per cent of world exports. The next most important region was the Far East, essentially the Philippines, which collectively supplied about 13 per cent of the world market. But the Far East does not sell to the European market and therefore does not really impinge on our story. The balance comes from Africa, primarily the Ivory Coast and the Cameroons, and from the Caribbean.

Among the importers, the two big blocs, the European Community and the USA are dominant. In 1993, each accounted for about 35 per cent of world imports, but in terms of value the EU share of the trade was appreciably greater (about 44 per cent in 1994[1]) because prices were – and remain – higher under the EU's regulated market than in the free market of the USA. Moreover, the USA is much closer to the main centres of production, so that shipping costs to the US market are much lower.

## Exporting Companies: The Big Three

Exports depend on refrigerated shipping and on sophisticated ripening and distribution facilities in the importing country. The trade is therefore capital-intensive and tends to be dominated by a few large companies.

The three big players on the world stage were, and remain, Chiquita (originally the United Fruit Company), Dole (originally Standard Fruit) and Del Monte, which together accounted for 64 per cent of world imports in 1994,[2] with Chiquita and Dole both having about 25 per cent and Del Monte 14 per cent. Though frequently described as 'multinationals', these three dominant companies were all US-based, although their trade in bananas and other produce was worldwide.

The creation of United Fruit (later Chiquita) in 1899 was described in Chapter 2. United Fruit was the largest operator in the field and grew rapidly. But having quickly established a dominant position, it was subsequently hauled before various tribunals over the years on charges of abusing it. Both Dole and Del Monte developed out of assets divested by United Fruit as a result of successive anti-trust actions.

The first was a congressional inquiry in 1908 following complaints by a competitor of abuses in Panama and Costa Rica. Following this inquiry, United Fruit voluntarily sold off a subsidiary, the Vaccaro Brothers Company, which became Standard Fruit and subsequently Dole.

In spite of this divestment, by 1954 United Fruit owned or controlled 85 per cent of the land in the American tropics suitable for banana cultivation, except for some in Ecuador.[3] Its power and influence were formidable. When the government of Guatemala, in pursuit of its land reform policy, sought to expropriate some of United Fruit's land, the Central Intelligence Agency (CIA) mounted a secret invasion of Guatemala, which led to the overthrow of the regime. According to a former vice-president of the company, 'United Fruit was involved at every level' of the operation.[4] Nevertheless, in the same year, the US government filed another anti-trust action against the company, which resulted in further divestment. This provided an opportunity for Del Monte to acquire United Fruit plantations in Guatemala and subsequently to become the third largest banana exporter.

But it was not only US institutions that challenged United Fruit's use of its commercial power. In 1976, the European Court of Justice found that Chiquita had abused its dominant position in the European market on a number of counts and most of their findings were upheld on appeal to the European Court of Justice in 1978.

United Fruit twice changed hands. In 1969 it was bought by AMK Sealed Caps, and renamed United Brands. AMK was owned by a financier, Eli Black, whose period of autocratic control proved disastrous both for United Brands and for himself. United Fruit's large financial reserves, which had attracted the takeover, were dissipated, assets were sold off, it lost market share and its share price plummeted.[5] At his wits' end, Eli Black threw himself out of the window of his 44th-floor office.

United Brands was rescued by a group of able chairmen and directors, who picked up the pieces and restored the share price from its nadir of $5 to $27. A major shareholder and participant in this revival was Carl Linder, who controlled the American Finance Corporation (AFC). In 1985 he took over United Brands and changed the company name to Chiquita, which was the brand name for its quality fruit.

Carl Lindner streamlined the company operations, disposing of a number of peripheral businesses that were not related to the mainstream banana trade. He decided to sell the Fyffes Group, the Company's UK subsidiary, because this did not fit well with a continental operation based on promotion of the Chiquita brand. Moreover, a large part of Fyffes' trade was importing bananas from the Caribbean. These imports depended on the high degree of protection provided by the UK national import regime. In 1986, EU governments made the commitment to a single market that would require such national regimes to be replaced before 1993 by a common regime for the whole European Community. Chiquita management at that time did not believe that the EU would be able and willing to impose a single market regime that would enable that trade to continue, even though the EU was committed to do so under the Lomé Convention. Chiquita therefore sold an 81 per cent stake in Fyffes to Fruit Importers of Ireland (FII) in the Irish Republic in 1986 and the balance three years later. So ended United Fruit's partnership with Elders and Fyffes that since 1902 had sustained Jamaica's export trade to the UK.

There was an unfortunate sequel to this amicable parting of the ways. In April 1990 a bitter conflict erupted between Fyffes and Chiquita in Honduras, where Chiquita had a contractual monopoly on exports. Fyffes sought to buy bananas at higher prices from an independent grower, but Chiquita won the support of the local court and of state troops, and bananas were forcibly unloaded from Fyffes' ships. As Fyffes' shipping manager ruefully remarked, 'in a banana republic, the big guys win'.[6] Nevertheless a compromise was brokered by the Honduras government, under which Fyffes was able to ship bananas from Honduras a year later.

Then in 1992 Chiquita sought to prevent Fyffes from using the Fyffes trademark name in continental Europe. But the European Commission ruled that this was an abuse of Chiquita's dominant position in the European market.

## Production in Latin America

All three dominant companies ran highly integrated operations in Latin America, either owning or controlling by contract much of the plantation production, except in Ecuador, as well as organising the shipping and marketing. The plantations were usually on very large areas of flat land often clustered around ports. Chiquita, for example, divided its plantations into divisions of typically 20,000 acres, each covering about twenty plantations, served by the company's own, self-contained communities of 30,000 to 40,000 people.[7]

Ecuador has been the world's largest exporter of bananas since at least the 1960s, except when production has been ravaged by climatic disasters. These are frequently caused by the dreaded El Niño, a warm current appearing off the west coast of Peru around Christmas time, which can result in severe changes of air pressure leading to storm damage and flooding. Ecuador supplies about 30 per cent of the world market, with the USA as its largest customer, and prides itself that production is not controlled by any of the three dominant companies, because of its restrictions on land ownership by foreign investors.[8] Dole and, to a lesser extent, Del Monte and Chiquita do buy and ship their bananas, but Bananera Naboa, an Ecuadorian company, is by far the largest shipper, with around 40 per cent of total banana exports. Production is carried out on about 5,000 farms, of which, in 1995, only 3 per cent exceeded 100 hectares (240 acres) and over a quarter did not exceed 5 hectares.

## Industrial Relations

Industrial relations have been one of the more disturbing aspects of the expanding banana industry in Latin America. There have been frequent complaints of workers having to put in very long hours at extremely low wages. Independent data are difficult to obtain, but it seems clear that Ecuador's pre-eminence as a low-cost producer partly reflects the generally lower level of wages paid to its workers on banana plantations. A US study in 2000 claimed that the average monthly wage for banana workers was US$56 in Ecuador, compared with $150–$200 in Honduras, $200–$300 in Colombia and $500 in Panama.[9] Three years later, a survey by the Latin American Workers' Union Co-ordination (COLSIBA), broadly confirmed this pecking order, with Panama paying the most and Ecuador almost the least, but showed a much higher wage level in Ecuador at $120 and much lower in Panama at $320 and thus a much smaller gap between Ecuador and others (see Figure 7.1). At the very bottom of the pile, Nicaragua's US$38 per month scarcely seems credible.

Companies have argued that wages are determined by the need to keep the export price of bananas below a given benchmark in order to stay in business against competitors, and that low wages are better than the unemployment that would occur if the business were taken elsewhere. That is the nub of the free-trade problem, to which we will return in Chapter 19.

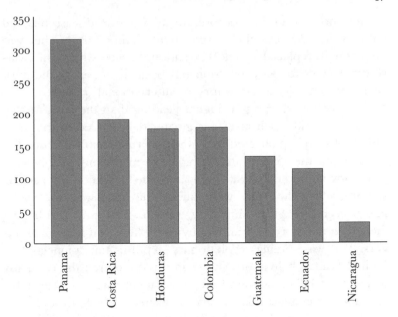

*Source*: COLSIBA (Latin American Co-ordination of Banana Workers' Unions), 2003.[10]

**Figure 8.1**   Wages of banana workers (US$/month)

Yet industrial relations problems embraced complaints not only of low wages but also of intimidation and physical violence against attempts to form trade unions and of lack of protection against spraying with harmful chemicals. This is a contentious area, but one campaigning body, Banana Link, has compiled a substantial catalogue of incidents that have occurred in various parts of Latin America. On the other hand, they have reported a marked improvement in recent years in the care some companies have taken to protect the environment.

## Major Changes in Production and Marketing

The banana export trade in Latin America was transformed in the 1960s and early 1970s by the need to abandon the banana plant most generally cultivated for export production, the Gros

Michel, because of its susceptibility to Panama disease (fusarial wilt), which destroys the root systems. The Gros Michel was increasingly replaced by the Cavendish variety, which was wilt-resistant. This forced conversion has been described as the most significant change in the history of international trade.[11]

The Cavendish variety is higher yielding than the Gros Michel and its fruit more delicate. This greater delicacy led to the revolutionary switch, pioneered by Standard Fruit, from exporting the bananas on the stem to exporting them in cartons. Stems were transported on overhead cableways from the field to central packing stations, where the hands were cut off the stem, washed, treated and packed into 40 pound (18 kg) cartons. The switch to boxing facilitated the move to branding by fixing labels on individual fingers. This was another revolutionary step, this time pioneered by United Fruit: labelling one finger in three required the company to print 2.5 billion stickers[12] and was labour-intensive, but it led to a greater emphasis on quality associated with the brand.

Measures to improve quality included covering stems while they were growing on the plant with plastic sleeves to prevent wind damage and scarring of the skin. Care was also taken in packing cartons to secure uniformity of finger length. All this required both substantial investment in equipment and a more labour-intensive operation. But the higher quality that it secured provided a market premium where that quality was associated with a specific brand name, such as Chiquita.

The FAO estimated in 1994 that the cost of equipping these plantations, including cableways and irrigation systems, could reach US$13,000 per hectare, over and above the cost of the land.[13] But the scale of the operations and the degree of vertical integration from plantation to market provide scope for substantial economies of scale.

A major consequence of the conversion from Gros Michel to Cavendish was that large areas of land under banana cultivation in Latin America became surplus to requirements because the new variety gave more than double the yield per hectare.[14] The United Fruit Company reduced its holdings of land in Latin America from 700,000 hectares in six countries in 1954 to 15,000 hectares in 1984 in only three – Honduras, Costa Rica and Panama.

### The ACP Scene

The industrial-type systems and vast plantations of Latin America contrast with the Windward Islands at the other extreme. Neither the hilly terrain nor the very small size of the farms lent themselves to mechanisation, and there was not the capital to install irrigation systems even in those locations where this was physically feasible. When boxing came, the cartons had to be carried on heads and backs to the nearest road and then be stacked on lorries. Because of the difficulty of maintaining uniform quality in those circumstances, boxes had to be re-sorted and repacked on arrival at ripening rooms in the importing country, thereby adding to costs. Similar problems arose in Jamaica.

But some other ACP countries were closer to the Latin American pattern, though still not able to compete with them on even terms. Both the Ivory Coast and Cameroon, with medium-size plantations and space for expansion, could produce at lower cost than either the Caribbean or Community growers. Both Chiquita and Dole had some involvement with production and marketing in these countries before the common market regime.

### The Race for the Community Market

The European Community obtains its bananas from four sources: Latin America, Africa, the Caribbean and from its own growers. Latin America is by far the most important source. In 1990, when restrictive import regimes still applied in half the member states of the Community, Latin America nevertheless accounted for 58 per cent of total Community supplies, Africa and the Caribbean together 18 per cent and Community growers 24 per cent.

The most striking feature of the world market at the time that the single market was being negotiated was the recent rapid rate of increase of both production and exports, particularly from Latin America. Latin American exports to the Community had remained fairly stable for many years at around 1.25 million tonnes. Then from 1986 to 1992 they increased by nearly 90 per cent to 2.4 million tonnes, in spite of the fact that access to the markets of half the member states was either closed or restricted.

This expansion was the result of both increased yields and a greater area planted. Some of the dominant trading companies were convinced that worldwide demand for bananas would rise. They saw three areas of potential growth: in Eastern Europe where liberalisation was expected to stimulate demand; in Asia, with the opening of access to Korea and with rising demand expected in other Asian countries; and, by no means least, in the European Community, where the introduction of the single market was expected to open up new opportunities. There appears to have been some wishful thinking that the Community would be unable or unwilling to meet its commitment to the ACP countries that they should be no worse off than before and that this failure would open up major new opportunities for dollar bananas.

Most of these expectations were disappointed. The one exception was in East Germany, where the collapse of the Berlin Wall had a phenomenal impact on banana consumption in Eastern Germany. Consumption soared from 3.9 kilo per head in 1989 to 18.1 in 1990 and a peak of 22.5 in 1992, far higher than anywhere else in Europe.[15] This seemed to reflect some special symbolic importance attached to the banana there, reminiscent of West Germany's insistence on exemption from the common tariff on bananas in the Treaty of Rome. But that level of consumption was not sustainable for long. There was little expansion elsewhere in Eastern Europe at that time and certainly not at remunerative prices. Expansion did occur in Asia, but much of this was filled locally by exports from the Philippines.

The European Community was potentially the richest prize, should the new common import regime open up hitherto restricted markets. The likely shape of the new European Community regime did not become known till 1992, when the Commission formally advanced its ideas for a quota regime, but the imminence of the single market had a major impact on companies' marketing policy. The leading companies jockeyed for position on the Community market. Each poured in supplies, almost regardless of return, in order to ensure that they had the highest possible base on which to stake a claim for quotas, if a quota system were introduced.

As a result, Latin American exports to the Community in 1992 were almost 20 per cent higher than in 1990. The higher supplies

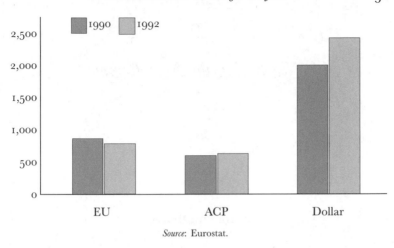

*Source*: Eurostat.

**Figure 8.2**   EU suppliers, 1990 and 1992 (1,000 tonnes)

caused a collapse in prices and financial losses all round. For 1992 Chiquita, the largest supplier, showed a loss of \$52 million in Europe, its most profitable market, compared to a profit of \$172 million the preceding year. Both Dole and Del Monte referred in their annual reports to the negative effect on the market of speculative trading ahead of the introduction of the regime, while Colombia claimed that its producers had suffered losses of \$70 million.

The oversupply and falling prices in 1992 reinforced the concerns of the ACP growers about the possible adverse effect of exposure to a single market. At the same time, those importing companies that had invested heavily in building up a higher market share were looking for a return in the form of freer access to those markets that had hitherto been restricted.

# 9

## Negotiating the New Regime

### The Challenge

It is hard to exaggerate the severity of the challenge facing the European Commission in having to devise a common banana regime. They had a duty under the Treaty of Rome to safeguard Community producers and under the Lomé Convention to ensure that traditional ACP suppliers were no worse off than in the past. Both the Community and the ACP countries were high-cost producers entirely dependent on the protection of restricted national markets in the Community. On the other hand, the Commission were constrained by the rules of the GATT (the General Agreement on Tariffs and Trade), which were then in the process of being reviewed; they were under pressure from several member states, led by Germany, to adopt a liberal regime; and they had to take account of consumer interests. Moreover, any proposal would have to secure the required majority vote in the Council of Ministers.

### Community Legislative Procedure

Under the Treaty of Rome setting up the European Community, it is the role of the Commission to propose legislation and that of the Council of Ministers to enact it. The Council can only change the Commission's proposal by unanimity, though in practice the Commission is an active partner in negotiations on draft legislation and will normally amend its proposal in a way likely to secure the necessary majority in the Council. Before making its decision, the Council must receive the opinion of the European Parliament, but is not constrained by it except in specified sectors, which do not include bananas.

The Council comprised ministers representing each of the then twelve member states, and their votes were weighted broadly according to population as shown below:

| | |
|---|---|
| France, Germany, Italy, UK | 10 votes each |
| Spain | 8 votes |
| Belgium, Portugal, Greece, Netherlands | 5 votes each |
| Ireland, Denmark | 3 votes each |
| Luxembourg | 2 votes |

To be adopted, a proposal had to have a 'qualified' majority of 54 votes out of the total of 76. A combination of 23 votes could therefore block a proposal. On bananas, the Council was split almost down the middle, with six of the twelve countries supporting a highly protective regime and five favouring a liberal regime, while one vacillated between the two views. There was likely to be a blocking minority against either approach.

The UK held the presidency of the Community during the last six months of 1992, when the adoption of the single market regime was due to be completed. The UK Minister of Agriculture, John Selwyn Gummer, who was in the chair, was personally committed to ensuring a satisfactory deal for the Caribbean and played a decisive role in securing the final settlement.

## Lobbying

Since as early as 1988, the Commission had been liberally supplied with conflicting advice and representations from interested parties, including member states, the Latin American producing counties, the ACP, the Caribbean and interested trading corporations. Chiquita probably led the field in the scale, vigour and persistence of its campaign for an unrestricted market. But on the opposing side, the Caribbean was fortunate in having Dame Eugenia Charles, Prime Minister of Dominica, spearheading its campaign. Eugenia

Charles is a large personality in every sense of the word and had a unique negotiating style, combining feminine emotional appeal with steely determination. A favourite opening gambit was, 'Why are you intent on destroying my country?', which placed more powerful interlocutors on the defensive. Nevertheless she went down well, even with top-flight, straitlaced intellectual males like Sir Leon Brittan, the European Trade Commissioner. But other Caribbean prime ministers also played vital, if less flamboyant, roles in the campaign. No one was left in any doubt of the crucial importance of banana exports to the Caribbean.

Technical backup was provided by the Caribbean Banana Exporters Association, a body representing the growers' organisations of the seven traditional Caribbean banana-exporting countries (Jamaica, Belize, Surinam and the four Windward Islands). This was originally formed in 1972 to promote cooperation on matters of common commercial interest such as research, but in 1988 it set up a London lobby, jointly with the three shipping companies, Fyffes, Geest and Jamaica Producers, to try to safeguard Caribbean interests in the negotiations for a single market regime.

## Proposals for the Regime

Under the Single Market Act of 1986, the Community was required to complete the single market for bananas, as for all other products, before 1 January 1993. Because of the anomalies of the Community banana market and the difficulty of devising an appropriate solution, bananas were the last item to be tackled. The Commission did not table its formal proposals until August 1992, but this was the culmination of a long period of exploratory work and discussions.

From the outset, the central problem for the Commission was how to safeguard Community and ACP growers in a single market, where they would be in competition from bananas from Latin America, produced at far lower cost than they could match. The Commission ruled out a system that permitted unrestricted entry subject only to the current 20 per cent tariff, because unlimited imports of low-priced Latin American bananas would drive both

Community and ACP producers out of the market, unless the Community were to accept an open-ended and probably unsustainable commitment to maintain their returns through some form of subsidy.

Instead the Commission proposed a solution based on quotas to limit imports of dollar bananas. The August proposals provided for an annual quota for Latin American bananas, to be set initially at 2 million tonnes, which was the average for recent years. ACP imports would also be limited to traditional quantities.

## Tariffication

The Commission proposal soon ran into difficulties. Some member states, led by Germany and the Netherlands, were opposed to any system of quotas for bananas. But there was also the problem that the proposed quota regime would not conform to the rules of the GATT and the Community would therefore have to seek a waiver for it. That would require the support of three-quarters of the GATT member countries and many member states thought this unlikely to be forthcoming, particularly since the USA and Latin American countries made clear their opposition to the Commission proposals.

In addition, the so-called Uruguay Round of multilateral trade negotiations was being held at that time. This was not finally concluded until the end of 1993 and would lead to the setting up of the World Trade Organisation (WTO) as well as agreement on a range of new measures designed to liberalise trade. Initially, this had not been expected to have a bearing on the EU regime, since bananas had not been included in its ambit, but just before Christmas 1991 the director-general, Arthur Dunkel, brought them into a compromise package that he put forward on agriculture. The main feature of that package was the concept of 'tariffication', namely that existing non-tariff barriers should be converted to tariff equivalents and both they and existing tariffs should be subject to reduction by 36 per cent in prescribed steps between 1993 and 1999.

This concept was gaining support and there was clearly something to be said for adopting a banana regime that would conform to principles being embodied in the new GATT round. The USA, for one, made clear its preference for a Community banana regime based on 'tariffication' rather than quotas, although it failed to fulfil a promise to send Mr Gummer its ideas on how this might operate.

But Caribbean governments were strongly opposed to replacing quotas by tariffs. Prime Minister Michael Manley of Jamaica urged both the president of the Commission and UK Prime Minister John Major not to go down that path. 'Jamaica and other ACP countries have consistently pointed out over the last two years that such an approach to the banana issue is unacceptable', he wrote to Commission president Jacques Delors in February 1992, 'in that it will leave the major relevant US multinationals free to use their financial muscle to make it impossible for Caribbean and other traditional ACP banana suppliers to sell bananas in the Community'.[1]

This view reflected a genuine fear that the dominant US corporations might be prepared to take losses for a period in order to drive the weakest suppliers out of the market, by pushing down prices with excessive supply. The events of 1991/92 (described in Chapter 8), when major corporations made huge losses in jockeying for position on the Community market, gave substance to those fears.

For the UK, the overriding objective was to secure a regime that met the needs of the Caribbean. The UK presidency saw the advantages of a tariff-based solution; the question was whether one could be devised which delivered the essential objective of safeguarding Caribbean and other ACP trade.

In the event, the UK presidency and the Commission together contrived a solution that was ingeniously simple. The Community had 'bound' in the GATT a tariff of 20 per cent for up to 1.4 million tonnes of third-country bananas. This was the rate applied to all non-ACP imports, except for those into Germany, which entered duty-free. The presidency proposal was to turn this into a tariff quota and for the tariff for imports outside that quota to be set at 850 ecus,[2] a level that was designed to be prohibitive and likely to remain so even after the progressive reductions to 1999. At the same time, the tariff quota rate was expressed as a fixed sum of 100 ecus, rather than 20 per cent *ad valorem*, which was broadly equivalent to it.

The difference between a tariff quota and a volume quota may seem rather fine, but it is crucial in GATT terms. For a straightforward volume quota puts an absolute limit on the volume that may be imported. A tariff quota merely puts a limit on the volume entitled to a tariff concession. If the full tariff rate is prohibitive, the practical effect may be the same. But in theory there is nothing to stop importers from exceeding a tariff quota, since they are entitled to enter the market by paying the higher tariff. The first challenge to the new regime in the GATT was to show the importance of this distinction.

Before launching this new approach, John Gummer, as UK Agriculture Minister as well as president of the Agriculture Council, was anxious to secure the agreement of the Caribbean, in view of their consistent opposition to tariffication hitherto. To this end, he made a hasty trip to the Caribbean just days before the December 1992 Council that was due to take the final decisions. In a series of meetings in Miami (with Belize), Jamaica and St Lucia, Caribbean ministers accepted that this was the best outcome that they could realistically hope for, and gave their support.

Yet the Caribbean had no say in the Council of Ministers and the move to tariffication did nothing to lessen the opposition of Germany and others opposed to a restrictive import regime. Germany was the most resolute opponent and had the most votes. They objected to losing their protocol privilege of duty-free entry and were genuinely concerned that the regime would lead to an unacceptable increase in prices to German consumers. They were also subject to powerful lobbying against the proposed regime by the US trade, notably Chiquita, which had a dominant position in the German market. Germany therefore opposed the proposal root and branch. But root-and-branch opposition is not a rewarding stance in a legislative system based on qualified majority voting, since it rules out the possibility of negotiating concessions of substance in return for your vote.

The presidency decided that the only prospect of securing agreement lay in the time-honoured Community device of making it part of a much larger package of agricultural measures, affecting products such as beef and milk and, above all, agro-monetary arrangements. The latter were provisions determining the special rates at which agricultural support prices, fixed in ecus, would be translated into national currencies. For some member states, the benefits attached to other elements of the package outweighed their objections to the proposals on bananas and led them to support the package as a whole. This secured, just, the necessary qualified majority. Although Germany voted against the package because of its opposition to the banana proposals, they were sufficiently concerned to secure the agro-monetary concessions in the package to refrain from leading any major attack on it in the Council. (For more background, see box, 'Packaging Votes', below.)

## Final Proposal

### ACP

The final agreement on the regime adopted by the Council provided for ACP bananas to enter duty-free up to a specified traditional quantity for each traditional supplier. Each country was allocated at least its best previous performance, resulting in a total of 857,000 tonnes, which was well in excess of their best collective performance in the past. Imports above these quotas would be at a preferential general tariff rate of 750 ecus. Since this rate was totally prohibitive for the ACP, this meant that in practice traditional ACP suppliers would for the first time face an effective volume limit on their exports to the Community.

### The B quota

Although the proposed tariff quota would enable import volumes into the Community to be controlled, there remained the problem of providing an incentive for importers to buy Community or ACP bananas, when much cheaper dollar bananas would become available in hitherto restricted parts of the Community. To meet this need, the Commission officials had originally proposed a form of 'partnership' or 'twinning' arrangement, for which precedents existed in the agriculture sector. This would have required part of the dollar quota to be earned by importing a specified proportion of ACP or Community bananas. But the details of the proposal were complex and nearly all member states saw it as a potential administrative nightmare.

The Commission therefore substituted the much simpler and more transparent proposal that 30 per cent of the 2 million tonne dollar quota be set aside for allocation to companies that had imported ACP or Community bananas during a rolling base period, initially 1989–91. The percentage set aside for this purpose was known as the B quota. Dollar bananas inevitably yielded more profit than those from ACP or Community origins, because they were bought at point of export at less than half the cost of ACP bananas yet would sell on the restricted Community market for the same price as ACP – or even at a premium over them. The B quota therefore provided a real incentive to importers to bring in ACP or Community bananas. The dollar licences thus earned enabled them to pay a viable price to ACP and Community growers.

It is not surprising that this proved the most contentious element of the regime. In addition, 3.5 per cent of the quota was set aside for newcomers who had not traded in bananas before 1992 (Category C), so that only 66.5 per cent of the quota remained for allocation to established dollar banana traders (Category A) in respect of their trade in the years 1989–91.

## Activity functions

The Commission added a further major complication. Because of wide divergences of commercial practices across the Community and the complexity of the banana trade, there was a risk of conflicting and overlapping claims for quota share in respect of the same consignments. The Commission therefore decided to determine entitlement to quota according to three different activities, namely:

- primary importer (an operator importing directly from country of origin and selling in the Community);
- secondary importer (an operator who acquires ownership of the bananas before their entry into the Community);
- ripener (as owner of the bananas).

More than one operator might be able to qualify under one or other of these heads in respect of the same consignment and an individual operator could qualify under more than one head for the same consignment. So entitlement was calculated on a points basis. The functions were weighted, after some political haggling, on a somewhat arbitrary basis, with 57 per cent attributed to primary import, 15 per cent for secondary import and 28 per cent for ripening. Whether this led to a more equitable distribution of quota is a moot point. It certainly added to the complexity of the regime and to its controversial nature.

The tariff quota system, combined with the cross-subsidy provided by the B quota, was considered enough to enable the ACP suppliers to maintain their position on the Community market. Each traditional ACP country had guaranteed access, duty-free, for a volume at least equal to the highest export level in recent times, while the total volume of dollar bananas was limited to 2 million tonnes, the level obtaining in 1990. The Commission and member states could reasonably claim that the regime thus fulfilled the Lomé commitment. The legislation provided for the regime to continue in operation until the expiry of the current Lomé Convention in February 2000, and for the position to be reviewed well before the end of that period.

## The UK Role

It is unlikely that this result would have been achieved if the UK had not been holding the presidency at that critical moment and the post of Minister of Agriculture occupied by a deeply religious politician with a strong moral commitment to securing a fair deal for Caribbean growers – a commitment illustrated, for example, in his reply to the select committee quoted at the end of Chapter 6. Only the dedication and drive of the presidency got the regime through.

It is interesting to speculate on what would have happened if the vote had failed – as it probably would have done if the banana regime had been voted on in isolation. The next two presidencies were successively Denmark and Belgium, both opponents of the regime. External factors, including the GATT case launched in 1993 against the existing restrictive national regimes, would probably have forced the Community eventually to adopt a common regime, as they were in any event pledged to do. But whatever finally emerged would have been very much less favourable to the Caribbean and other ACP countries, though possibly less controversial in the GATT.

The support that the regime did provide to the ACP would in any event rapidly be eroded as a result of attacks on it that started even before the regime came into operation.

## A Voting Crisis

But the regime very nearly failed to get off the ground. The agricultural package, including bananas, secured the necessary qualified majority in the last Agriculture Council of the UK presidency in December 1992, with support, albeit reluctant in some cases, from all member states except Germany, Denmark and Portugal, who each voted against. That Council, however, only set out the agreement of principle on bananas. That needed to be translated into the necessary legislation.

This was put to the Council in February 1993 under the next presidency, that of the Danes, who had strongly opposed the tariff quota regime and voted against the deal. Nevertheless the legislation should have commanded the necessary majority from those who supported the December agreement. Unfortunately, Belgium and the Netherlands, having pocketed the other elements of the package, then switched their votes, following criticism in their countries. This would have scuppered the regime, leaving the implementing legislation one vote short of the qualified majority. John Gummer, who had steered through the agreement, is said to have expressed his views on this betrayal in terms more forthright than was customary in the restrained environment of ministerial council meetings, but to no avail.

Rescue came from an unlikely quarter. The Danes had strongly opposed the proposals for the regime and voted against them. But the Danish Agriculture Minister, as president of the Council, insisted that the Community could not operate if ministers went back on agreements in that way. He therefore had Denmark's vote cast in favour in order to get the legislation through – an act of rare altruism, for which Danish banana traders never forgave him.

## Challenge from Germany

Germany, however, remained determined in its continued opposition to the regime. It challenged its legality in the European Court of Justice and sought an injunction from the Court to stop the regime coming into operation until the case had been heard. This was refused and the regime was initiated on 1 July 1993 in accordance with the Council legislation. A year later the Court issued its judgment upholding the legality of the regime. It sympathised with the German view on specific elements, in particular that the dollar quota should have been somewhat larger, but did not regard this as sufficient cause to justify the Court condemning the legislation.

## Extra Support for Community Growers

There was one crucial difference under the new regime between the arrangements for ACP growers and those in the Community. In addition to the external measures of support provided by the regime, Community growers were to receive a direct subsidy to make up any difference between average market returns and a predetermined benchmark. This was to ensure that banana growers obtained support comparable to that for other agricultural products. This major additional benefit for Community growers gave effect to the key principle of Community preference set out in the Treaty of Rome.

The Commission had also proposed a form of temporary income support for the ACP to operate as a safety net were the regime to fail initially to sustain the market as intended. The Commission argued that a sudden loss of revenue would impact particularly severely on small producers and that compensation should be paid to directly to them. However, the UK opposed the principle of income support for the ACP, and with the leading protagonist for the Caribbean opposed there was no prospect of its adoption. Instead an aid package was subsequently provided for approved programmes of restructuring and improvements.

It was the then Overseas Development Administration (since replaced by the Department for International Development) that took the lead in opposing any form of income support, even in case of unexpected market collapse. This was not, in their view, an appropriate use of aid funds. But this contrasted starkly with UK proposals in 1990 in a 'Discussion Paper' on a future regime, which had proposed transitional and degressive subsidies for Community and ACP producers.

It was an unfortunate decision. In the event, the market did collapse following the introduction of the regime, in the last quarter of the year, due largely to mismanagement of the quota. For that period, the deficiency payments paid to Community producers amounted in some cases to nearly half their income. The ACP growers received no income support and suffered severely. The programme for medium-term restructuring and improvement aid was no help to small growers whose income was cut as a result of this collapse.

This illustrated the gulf between the support for banana growers in Dominica and St Lucia and that for their next-door neighbours in Martinique and Guadeloupe, who in 1946 had voted to become provinces (départements) of France rather than independent states. The protection of these French growers in the Caribbean remained throughout the overriding objective of French policy on bananas. To this end, France had a tactical alliance with the UK on banana policy for most of the time until the final crisis, when French policy and Caribbean needs sharply diverged.

However, the immediate problem for the Community and ACP alike was the challenge immediately launched by Latin American countries, with US encouragement and support, against the newly agreed regime.

## Packaging Votes

The practice of collating measures into packages for voting
dates back to the period when each member state had a right
of veto on virtually everything, so that agreement on any piece
of legislation required unanimity. Members frequently withheld
agreement on one agricultural item in order to secure concessions on another. As a result, virtually all significant decisions on
agriculture were combined into one vast annual package, which
offered goodies to everybody and was presented for acceptance
or rejection as a whole. With the removal of the veto on agricultural issues, decision-making is usually quicker and more
subtle. The presidency will try to secure a qualified majority
on a particular piece of legislation by negotiating concessions
to swing votes. It will not waste them on those who would vote
against whatever concessions were offered.

The Council Secretariat, which is the authority on this issue,
maintains that a delegation can vote in favour of a package yet
abstain on or vote against a particular element in the package.
This would be recorded in the minutes. But according to those
involved, this did not appear to be widely understood at the
time that the regime was negotiated and was not reflected in
the way that ministers acted.

Fortuitously, putting the banana deal in a package had the
opposite effect for Portugal, which favoured a restricted market
for bananas, but voted against the package because it was dissatisfied with other elements.

The Danish altruism in switching sides in order to ensure
that what had been agreed was implemented was rare in the
Community but not unique. Harold Wilson's much-vaunted 'renegotiation' of the terms of entry following the Labour victory
of 1974 achieved very little. But one significant concession was to
improve terms of access for New Zealand butter. Luxembourg,
a major exporter of dairy products, was one of several bitter
opponents of that deal. But as the Presidency it insisted that
the implementing legislation must be pushed through.

# 10

# The First GATT Challenges, 1993–94

## The GATT

The General Agreement on Tariffs and Trade was set up following the Second World War in response to a widespread view among developed countries that the trade restrictions of the 1930s had reduced prosperity and that the world would benefit from lower tariffs and trade liberalisation. An initial 23 countries signed the Agreement in 1947. By 1995, when the new WTO took over a revised GATT, there were 128 member states (contracting parties), accounting for 90 per cent of world trade.

The key principle of the GATT is non-discrimination. It lays down a complex set of rules governing trade between its members. Each contracting party is entitled to receive Most Favoured Nation status from all other member states. So one member must not be treated more or less favourably than another. Thus Article I of the GATT prohibits any preferential treatment of one member over another in respect of customs duties or any import or export charges; and Article XIII bans discrimination between members in the administration of any form of quantitative restriction (including tariff quotas). Article XI prohibits quantitative restrictions, except in certain narrowly defined circumstances.

The GATT is also committed to progressively reducing barriers to trade. Each country acceding to the GATT sets out a schedule of concessions on rates of import duties on specific goods negotiated with their principal trading partners. These rates, which are often limited to a specific total volume of imports, then apply equally to all GATT members exporting the goods concerned to that country. These tariff rates are thus 'bound' and can only be changed under procedures laid down in Article XXVIII, which imply the negotiation of appropriate concessions. (A case in point is cited in Chapter 5 above, when in 1956 the UK negotiated an increase in British import duties on bananas, which were 'bound' to Brazil, conceding in exchange the removal of UK duties on brazil nuts.)

## The First Challenge

In the autumn of 1992 five Latin American banana-exporting countries, Colombia, Costa Rica, Guatemala, Nicaragua and Venezuela, requested initial discussions in the framework of the GATT on the Community's proposed new common market regime for bananas, but the Community refused to enter into formal consultations on a regime that did not yet exist. However, on 8 February 1993 the Community did agree to a request by those countries for a GATT panel to consider whether the five restrictive national regimes that the common regime was due to replace were compatible with GATT rules. A three-man panel of trade experts was duly appointed. Because this was a case brought by developing countries, a special accelerated procedure was applied, which had been agreed in 1996 for disputes involving developing countries. The panel reported in nine weeks, submitting its report on 19 May.

In view of the basic rules of the GATT, described above, it was hardly surprising that the panel found both the quantitative restrictions imposed by France, Italy, UK, Spain and Portugal and the tariff preferences granted to the ACP to be in breach of the GATT. Indeed, the panel implied that the Community had added insult to injury in extending the tariff preferences to some ACP countries that were not even GATT members.

The Community urged various arguments in defence of the regimes, including that the complainants were debarred from objecting by having knowingly acquiesced in the measures for many years (the principle of 'estoppel'). But the panel did not accept that failure by one party to invoke a right at a particular point in time could be regarded as releasing other contracting parties from their obligations.

The panel also rejected a Community argument that the quantitative restrictions were exempt under the so–called 'grandfather clause'. This was a provision in the Protocols of Provisional Accession to the GATT signed by the original contracting parties in 1947. This bound each state to apply the agreement provisionally 'to the fullest extent not inconsistent with its legislation existing on the date of the Protocol'. The panel pointed out that this provision was intended as a temporary measure, to avoid delays in accession while acceding countries made necessary changes to mandatory domestic legislation. The panel did not believe that it should be invoked forty years later as a defence for measures that were in any event not mandatory on the governments concerned.

An attempt by the Community to argue that the Lomé Convention was a free-trade area agreement and thereby exempt from breach of Article I also failed on the grounds that a free-trade area agreement required reciprocity between the parties, which Lomé specifically did not entail. On the contrary, the purpose of Lomé was for the Community to confer benefits on the ACP countries to aid their development, without comparable concessions on the part of the ACP.

The adverse panel ruling in this case was largely academic since, by the time of its final report, the regimes in question were about to expire. But the rulings were unwelcome precedents, which could be cited by later panels. Moreover, this panel was swiftly followed by a request from the same countries for a panel on the new single market regime. In the light of the first panel ruling, the second panel inevitably found against key elements of the new common market regime.

## The Second Challenge

To start with, the panel upheld an objection by the complainants against the new in-quota tariff of 100 ecus per tonne. The previous duty of 20 per cent *ad valorem* had been bound in the Community's schedule of concessions under the GATT. The panel ruled that the new fixed rate could potentially prove higher than 20 per cent; and that any change from the bound rate must be negotiated under the special procedures provided for this purpose (Article XXVIII).

More fundamentally, the panel ruled, like its predecessor, that the tariff preference for the ACP, giving them duty-free entry, was contrary to Article I, since it manifestly gave some members preferential terms of entry denied to other members. The Community again urged, among other arguments, that Lomé represented a free-trade area and was therefore exempt, but this was again rejected.

The panel also ruled that the allocation of part of the tariff quota to importers of Community or ACP bananas (the B licence system) was contrary to the GATT. By giving incentives to import from certain origins, it discriminated between contracting parties, contrary to the requirements of Article I; and the same incentives similarly favoured domestic producers over third countries, thereby breaching Article III.4.

Thus two crucial elements in the system of protection for the ACP were ruled to be contrary to the GATT. The Community did win, however, on one very important point. The panel rejected arguments by the complainants that the tariff quota, combined with the prohibitive out-of-quota tariff, amounted to a quantitative restriction and was therefore incompatible with the GATT, which precludes quantitative restrictions (Article XI). The panel pointed out that the system of concessionary tariff quotas, with a higher tariff for quantities above those quotas, was widely adopted in the GATT. It ruled that 'the mere fact that the level of the [higher] tariff may be such as to make imports of bananas subject to the tariff unprofitable does not turn the tariff into a quantitative restriction'. The subtle logic of this argument was that governments cannot control the market impact of their measures, and the legality of those measures cannot therefore be made subject to something so unpredictable as their trade effect. This ruling fully vindicated the UK presidency's decision to switch to a tariff quota system in place of the straightforward quota previously proposed.

Nevertheless, the overall panel ruling, if adopted, would have destroyed the regime, with disastrous consequences for ACP banana growers in Africa and the Caribbean. But under the GATT rules then obtaining, a panel report was only enforceable if and when the GATT Council adopted it. The accepted convention was for adoption to be by consensus. With Community and ACP members opposed, that consensus was not forthcoming for either of these panel reports.

It seems extraordinary that panel rulings could be rendered inoperative in this way, however welcome the convention may have been in this instance to the Community and the ACP. But this was about to change. The new World Trade Organisation (WTO), agreed upon in April 1994 in the Uruguay Round negotiations, would be armed with much greater powers for settling disputes. The threat to the Community regime was therefore deferred, not overcome.

Yet the panel did offer a constructive suggestion for the way forward. In its concluding statement, the panel stated that it 'was well aware of the economic and social effects of the EEC measures on the ACP banana exporting countries'. However, the rules of the GATT had to be applied and the proper course was to use those provisions of the GATT 'that are designed to allow Contacting Parties to take into account, in the view of the panel, economic and social considerations'. The way forward, in other words, was to seek a waiver (under Article XXV.5) providing exemption from the rules on economic and social grounds. A waiver would require widespread support within the GATT: three-quarters of votes cast, with the majority representing more than half the total of GATT members. Nevertheless, the Community did pursue that course, among others, to strengthen its position following the adverse panel report.

## 11

# The Birth of the WTO:
# Compromise at Marrakesh

### The Uruguay Round

Negotiations began in 1986 to secure agreement among trading nations on measures to reduce both tariff and non-tariff barriers to international trade. This complex series of negotiations lasted seven years. It was only driven to a conclusion by the imminent expiry of the time-limited 'fast track' power that Congress had conceded to the US President authorising him to sign an agreement that they had not scrutinised. One such authority conferred on Republican President George Bush (senior) expired before agreement was reached. His Democratic successor, Bill Clinton, managed to obtain a new fast-track power from Congress, but only till the end of April 1994. This meant that the negotiations proper would have to be complete by mid-December 1993 if the necessary Final Acts were to be ready in time for signature in April – at the special session to be held at Marrakesh.

Only the drive and determination of the conference chairman, Peter Sutherland, a former European Commissioner recently appointed director-general of the GATT, enabled this deadline to be met. At 7.30 p.m. on 15 December 1993 he brought down the final gavel to a standing ovation.[1]

Although slow and sometimes moribund, the Uruguay Round brought about the biggest ever reduction in tariffs. It provided for the GATT to be replaced from 1 January 1995 by a new World Trade Organisation which was endowed with a much strengthened mechanism for settling disputes between members. Most important was the reversal of the old GATT convention requiring panel reports to be adopted by consensus. In future panel rulings would be deemed adopted unless rejected by consensus.

The GATT rules governing international trade in goods were retained as an integral part of the WTO but additional agreements were added to cover other areas, including intellectual property rights and, significantly for the banana dispute, a General Agreement on Trade in Services (GATS). The GATS extended to services the GATT principles of most Favoured Nation treatment applying, without any form of discrimination, to all WTO members.

A ministerial meeting was held in Marrakesh, Morocco, in April 1994 for signature of the Final Act of the Round, incorporating the detailed agreements. During the negotiations some Latin American countries indicated that they were unwilling to support the new order unless their concerns over the EU's banana regime were met. This may have carried some weight given the GATT tradition of agreements being reached by consensus and a widespread understanding that the Latin Americans had the backing of the USA. But the European Commission was in any event anxious to resolve the issue if it could. Although the GATT panel reports had not been adopted, they constituted a present embarrassment and a threat for the future.

The EU therefore tried to strike a deal with the complainants and at Marrakesh reached agreement with four out of the five Latin American countries: Costa Rica, Colombia, Nicaragua and Venezuela. But Guatemala would not play ball. Nevertheless, when the four countries announced their acceptance of the EU offer, the Community made clear at Marrakesh its willingness to seek solutions with other interested parties in order to be able to maintain, without disruption, their means of helping the ACP.

## The Banana Framework Agreement

Under the deal, known as the Banana Framework Agreement (BFA), the consenting four countries agreed not to press for adoption of the panel report or to bring any further complaints during the lifetime of the regime. In return they received concessions that

**Table 11.1**   Quotas: BFA allocation and actual share (%)

|  | Actual share | | BFA allocation |
|---|---|---|---|
|  | 1989/91 | 1992 |  |
| Colombia | 20.4 | 21.5 | 21.0 |
| Costa Rica | 25.3 | 19.2 | 23.4 |
| Nicaragua | 2.2 | 1.1 | 3.0 |
| Venezuela | 0.0 | 0.0 | 2.0 |

*Source*: European Commission, *Report on the Operation of the Banana Regime*, 1995.

significantly reduced the protection afforded to the ACP but also complicated the operation of the regime. These were: an increase in the tariff quota from 2 million tonnes to 2.1 million in 1994 and 2.2 million in 1995; a reduction of the in-quota tariff from 100 ecus to 75; and the allocation of specific percentages of the tariff quota to each of the four countries.

The last of these provisions proved highly controversial. The quota allocations were apparently based on average export performance in 1989–91, which, surprisingly, was the latest period for which figures were available. Comparing the allocations with each country's performance in that period and also in 1992, they do not seem particularly generous, except to the two very minor suppliers, as Table 11.1 shows.

The allocations guaranteed access to the beneficiary countries but they also, in principle, imposed a limit. However, the BFA enabled any unused balance from one member's allocation to be reallocated among the others. Collectively, the BFA thus reserved half of the whole dollar quota to these four countries. This rendered the deal unacceptable to those who were not party to it and saw their potential exports correspondingly reduced – and none more so than Ecuador, which was about to become a member of the WTO.

The EU had invited Ecuador to participate in the BFA with an allocation of 20 per cent of the tariff quota. This exactly reflected Ecuador's performance in 1989–91. But Ecuador had massively increased its exports in 1991 and 1992 and in the latter year accounted for 28 per cent of the EU's dollar imports. As an expanding and highly competitive producer, it saw this offer as a constraint rather than an assurance and turned it down.

The allocation of specific quota shares to the four countries made life much more difficult and costly for importing companies. The organisation of shipping programmes is a complex business, which requires planning and commitments long in advance if costs are to be kept to a minimum. But the arbitrary country limits imposed by the BFA added a significant new element of uncertainty, since shippers would have to adjust their schedules to fit in with the export quota availability in any country at a particular time.

Moreover, the Agreement entitled each of the four signatory countries to issue 'special export certificates' for up to 70 per cent of their allocation. This would permit them to impose a charge for the certificates, thus securing for themselves some of the 'quota rent' generated by the tariff quota system. (The reason for limiting export certificates to 70 per cent was to exempt the 30 per cent B quota, designed to cross-subsidise the ACP, from bearing any supplementary charge.) The provision for export certificates was potentially a real financial benefit to the exporting country, but a corresponding loss to the companies trading with it. On top of this, the need to match import licences with those export certificates placed a significant additional burden on the companies concerned.

## The Effect on ACP

The ACP countries were not consulted before the BFA deal was reached, although under the terms of the Lomé Agreement they should have been. The deal was intended to serve the interests of both ACP and EU growers in ending the dispute, but it manifestly clawed back some of the safeguards bestowed by the regime in fulfilment of the Lomé commitment. The reduction on the tariff was unwelcome but far less damaging than the increases in the tariff quota, which seriously threatened the stability of the market. There had already been a collapse in prices towards the end of 1993, because teething troubles in the introduction of the regime led to oversupply. A 10 per cent quota increase was the last thing that was needed at that stage.

However, the European Commission had sweeteners to offer in partial compensation. The Dominican Republic was an ACP country that had only recently started exporting to the Community on a substantial scale. It did not therefore qualify as a traditional ACP supplier. Following much lobbying by the Dominican Republic, the Marrakesh Agreement had allocated 90,000 tonnes out of the tariff quota for 'non-traditional' imports from the Dominican Republic and other ACP countries. This helped to relieve particular problems not only of the Dominican Republic, but also of Ghana, Belize, the Ivory Coast and Cameroon.

The Banana Framework Agreement totally failed to achieve its objective of securing peace and tranquillity for the regime. Four countries had been bought off, but at the cost of reducing protection for the ACP and of alienating other Latin American countries and, most significantly, of provoking the USA. For the world's largest banana trader, Chiquita, the BFA was the last straw. Chiquita started to exercise its considerable political muscle to bring down both that Agreement and the entire banana import regime. To this end they turned to the US government, which itself indicated, at a later date, that it resented the BFA more than any other element of the EU banana regime.

# 12

# Chiquita and the US Campaign

## Why Chiquita Felt Aggrieved

Chiquita, a publicly owned US company, was at the time the world's largest banana trader, with just over 25 per cent of world trade.[1] Bananas accounted for about 60 per cent of its total revenue, the balance coming from other fresh and prepared foods.

About two-thirds of the bananas Chiquita traded were grown on land it owned or leased in Latin America, primarily in Panama, Costa Rica, Honduras and Colombia. The balance was bought directly from growers under contract. Chiquita thus operated a highly integrated and cost-efficient system from plantation to market. There were, however, claims of worker exploitation on the plantations, with low wages and inadequate safeguards against health hazards from aerial spraying.

Chiquita had invested heavily during the late 1980s in expanding production in Latin America and increasing its shipping resources. That expansion was financed largely by loan and was motivated by perceived prospects for growth in Eastern Europe and Asia as well as in the EU. Dole, the second largest trader, likewise invested in expansion. As a result, exports to the EU from Latin America rose every year from 1989 onwards – from 1.4 million tonnes in 1987 to 2.37 million tonnes in 1992.

However, production far outstripped growth in demand. The result was a severe fall in prices in oversupplied markets. As we saw in Chapter 8, this was particularly sharp in the EU, where all three dominant traders were striving to be best placed for whatever new regime was adopted from 1993, including the possibility of import quotas. Margins fell and Chiquita registered a loss of over $52 million in Europe in 1992, compared to a peak profit of $172 in 1991. Given the high debt that the company had to service on their investment in expansion, dividends had to be cut. This led to the collapse of its share price from nearly $50 to $10.

Chiquita blamed the new EU regime for its woes. It was 'a sweeping expropriation of US interests for the benefit of foreign firms'.[2] The quota of 2 million tonnes represented a cut of 20 per cent on the company's actual imports in 1992 and therefore reduced its potential market, while the B licence system effectively transferred its trade to European companies by granting 30 per cent of the dollar quota to importers of ACP and EU bananas.[3] Chiquita claimed that these factors together entailed a 65 per cent loss in its EU market share. In addition, the restriction on imports into the EU by means of the tariff quota had resulted in greater volumes having to be sent to other markets, consequently reducing prices and profits in those markets as well.

Chiquita also maintained that the regime had, through the unfair allocation of import licences, disrupted its long-standing relationships with its trade customers and undermined the basis of its investments in its dedicated shipping fleet of fourteen re-frigerated vessels.

It is not difficult to understand these complaints. The combined effect of the B licence system and of allocating a share of the licences to secondary importers and ripeners was to leave Chiquita with a licence provision well below the level of past imports. This did not necessarily prevent Chiquita from making those imports, but it inevitably strengthened the negotiating hand of its trading partners in Europe, who now held some of the licences. In addition, the limit on the total volume of imports could well have undermined investment plans based on continuing growth.

Moreover, Chiquita was rebuffed in attempts it made in the summer of 1994 to contract for all or part of the trade in Windward Island bananas, which would have brought it the benefits of the B licences. But this would have required the islands to end their existing exclusive contract with Geest and place their future in the hands of a company that had hitherto been the leading opponent of a protective regime. This was a leap in the dark that they could not contemplate.

Chiquita had encouraged and supported the Latin American complainants in the two GATT cases (see Chapter 10), but, although the Latin Americans had won, Chiquita was no better off because the panel reports had not been adopted. The old GATT system had enabled the EU and the ACP to prevent the consensus necessary for adoption.

Then came the Banana Framework Agreement negotiated at Marrakesh. For Chiquita, this was the last straw. The company claimed that the Agreement 'establishes arbitrary and disruptive sourcing requirements; authorises confiscatory and discriminatory licences and fees; and, since its signing, has worked a substantial incremental hardship on US commercial interests.'[4]

## The US Trade Act

Chiquita therefore launched the formal machinery of a petition to the United States Trade Representative (USTR) under Section 301 of the US Trade Act of 1974. It did so jointly with the Hawaii Banana Industry Association, the only banana growers' body in the USA. Hawaiian production was small, but for the purposes of Section 301 it was important to show that US workers were affected by the trade practices at issue.

Section 301 required the USTR to investigate the complaint and, if appropriate, to take action where measures by other countries were damaging US trade. This case was unprecedented, however, because it concerned a product that was not a US export but exported from other countries by a US company.

## Caribbean Reaction

The petition directly embroiled the US government in a dispute over the EU banana regime. It consequently forced Caribbean governments into direct confrontation with the USA, because, in the course of its Section 301 investigation, the USTR threatened sanctions against the EU aimed at dismantling the regime on which the Caribbean states depended for their economic survival.

Those threatened by the 301 proceedings challenged in written submissions to the USTR both the Chiquita case and the claim made by USTR that US companies had 'lost hundreds of millions of dollars' as a consequence of the EU regime. Rebuttals were made by individual companies, by trade associations and, at political level, by the governments of the fourteen member states of the Caribbean Economic Community (Caricom).

These rebuttals argued that it was difficult to understand the claim of huge losses by US companies because:

- The main losses of Chiquita were sustained in 1992 before the regime came into operation in mid-1993. Their accounts showed that they were back in profit in Europe in 1993 at $78.7 million and in 1994 at $73.7 million, not as high as in the boom years of 1990 and 1991 but a great deal better than the heavy losses of 1992.
- Chiquita's loss of market share also *preceded* the introduction of the regime, falling from a highly unprofitable peak in mid-1992 to below its 1990 level at the beginning of 1993.
- The other major US company, Dole, which had virtually the same share of the world market as Chiquita, had not joined the petition and had made no complaint. It had adapted its marketing and investment policy to fit in with the EU regime, including taking a substantial stake in the ACP and EU trade. As a result it had *increased* its market share in the EU by four percentage points since 1990.

On a more political plane, Caribbean governments seized every possible occasion to stress to the US administration at the highest levels the threat that the attack on the regime posed to their vulnerable economies. The issue was raised at the US–Caribbean summit in Miami in December 1994; in subsequent letters to President Clinton from prime ministers of many of the states of Caricom; and in a meeting between the chairman of Caricom, Prime Minister Esquivel of Belize, and deputy US trade representative Ambassador Barchefsky in March 1995.

## The US Viewpoint

The US Administration saw the banana dispute in the broader context of a series of trade disputes with the EU. These covered not only bananas but also hormones in beef and, subsequently genetically modified foods, where European sensitivities on issues affecting health and the environment clashed with US dedication to the rights of US companies to free trade.

Moreover, the USA had always taken a sceptical view of claims that the principles of free trade should be modified to meet inherited obligations of former imperial powers. In his biography of Winston Churchill, the late Roy Jenkins cites the historic meeting in 1941 between Roosevelt and Churchill that paved the way to the Atlantic Charter. Churchill had the greatest difficulty in persuading Roosevelt to modify the proposed commitment to 'access on equal terms to the trade and raw materials of the world' with the qualification 'with due respect for existing obligations'.[5]

The USA was prepared to accept a degree of tariff preference to help Caribbean and other ACP countries, but no other form of discrimination in the treatment of trading partners. In its eyes, the EU had deliberately chosen a means of meeting their obligations to the ACP that helped EU operators at the expense of US traders. The USA was determined that, in this case, 'Europe should not be allowed to get away with it.' It was not inhibited in this approach by any overriding concern for the consequences for the Caribbean, since the end of the Cold War had greatly diminished the political significance of Caribbean states to the US government.

Moreover, the USA was at pains to point out, while the EU market might be critical to small Caribbean countries, the main beneficiaries of the 'discriminatory and burdensome' regime were other ACP countries, which the USA considered better able to compete with Latin America, and the Community's own producers.

Accordingly, the US response to representations from aggrieved Caribbean governments was robust and unyielding. The USA insisted that it had no desire or intention to harm the Caribbean; but the EU should not seek to honour its Lomé commitments at the expense of US commercial interests. The responsibility lay with the EU to find other means of doing so. Over time, the USTR offered plenty of advice on how the EU might do this (see Chapter 15).

The USA also argued that the EU regime was a highly inefficient and wasteful means of aiding the Caribbean. ACP growers could not continue indefinitely to rely on that degree of protection; it would therefore be in the interest of the growers themselves for the regime to be replaced by direct aid to finance phasing out the less efficient producers.

## USA Launches Attack in WTO

USTR demanded that the Community make radical changes to the regime, by substantially increasing the tariff quota and cutting the B licences by 90 per cent. This would have eliminated effective support for the ACP. When it became clear that this would not be negotiable, the then US trade representative, Mickey Kantor, decided to pursue the issue in the WTO, rather than attempt to impose sanctions unilaterally. To facilitate this, he terminated the 301 action initiated by Chiquita in September 1995 and opened a new one on his own initiative on the same day.

The purpose of this manoeuvre was to gain time and flexibility to launch a case in the WTO. Otherwise he would have had to announce a conclusion on the original petition by 17 October 1995 and would have been under pressure, particularly from leading Republicans, to take retaliatory action unilaterally. The new, autonomous, 301 action required a determination after the WTO proceedings had ended or on 27 March 1997, whichever was earlier. This therefore provided both the space for action in the WTO and a fall-back option if that action was unsuccessful or delayed.

## Costa Rica and Colombia

At the same time the USTR launched a Section 301 action against Costa Rica and Colombia over their participation in the Banana Framework Agreement with the European Union, demanding their withdrawal from it. In the event, USTR withdrew their case in January 1996 in return for minor technical changes in the way the offending states administered the Agreement and promises that they would seek to persuade the EU to adopt a more liberal approach. This was essentially a face-saving formula which the press in Costa Rica rightly greeted as a victory, particularly in the light of an extraordinary attempt by the Republican Senate Majority Leader Senator Dole to secure penal sanctions against those countries remaining in the Banana Framework Agreement.

Bob Dole was close to Carl Lindner, the boss of Chiquita, who later placed his personal jet at Dole's disposal for his campaign for the presidential nomination. Senator Dole sought to back up the 301 action against Colombia and Costa Rica by introducing a Bill into the Senate to deprive them of all trade preferences if they did not renounce the Banana Framework Agreement with the European Community. This would have deprived them of the preferences they enjoyed under the GATT Generalised System of Preferences for developing countries, from the benefits of the Caribbean Basin Initiative[6] and from the Andean Trade Preference Act. The latter was granted in 1991 by the Republican Bush ad-ministration to compensate Colombia for efforts to eradicate nar-cotic crops. This was therefore a very heavy-handed threat. The Dole bill did not pass, but it cast a revealing light on the extent of Chiquita's political influence.

## Other US Companies

One striking feature of the 301 proceedings was the lack of support for USTR from the other major US companies. In both of the 301 actions against the EU, Dole submitted to USTR specific proposals for a compromise. These were based on the 'need to move, in the long term, to a more open market banana regime in line with GATT principles' together with 'recognition that precipitous change in current trading arrangements would cause a disproportionate amount of harm to ACP and European banana producing regions.'[7] These proposals were not taken up by USTR.

Del Monte went further, issuing a public statement of support for the EU regime. 'Del Monte modified its production, transportation and distribution systems to accommodate changes in view of the new regulations. Del Monte is faithfully working within the system and the company will continue to support [it].'

## The Role of Political Donations

The US press speculated openly about a possible link between the US government backing for Chiquita and the generous political donations made by Carl Lindner, chairman of the holding company owning Chiquita.[8] Lindner had long made political donations, primarily to the Republican Party. But he also forged links with the Democratic administration of Bill Clinton. *Time* magazine noted that the day after the US trade representative took the issue to the WTO on 11 April 1996, Lindner and his top officials began funnelling more than $500,000 to Democratic Party coffers in about two dozen states. In the period from 1990 to 1997, Lindner and his companies were said to have distributed $2 million between the two political parties.[9] Like other top donors, he received red-carpet treatment at the White House, including a night in the Lincoln bedroom. It is hardly surprising that people asked whether this largesse led the administration to give greater impetus and priority to the battle over bananas than might otherwise have been considered appropriate for a product that the USA did not export.

# The First WTO Case

The case that finally went to a WTO panel in May 1996 was based on a complaint filed by the USA, Honduras, Guatemala, Mexico and Ecuador, now a WTO member, but was led and inspired by the USA. The panel reports[1] that resulted provide an illuminating analysis of the depth and scope of the GATT rules on non-discrimination and of the new agreement on services (GATS).

## A New Ball Game

As indicated in Chapter 11, major changes had occurred since the previous GATT panels. The creation of the WTO, which replaced the GATT, instituted a new, much more effective, dispute settlement procedure, which greatly benefited complainants by making adoption of panel rulings automatic. Meanwhile, the battle lines had changed with the withdrawal from the fray of the four Latin American signatories of the Banana Framework Agreement (BFA). However, the BFA itself was a major bone of contention, while the quiescence of the BFA signatories was offset by the recruitment to the US side of Ecuador, the world's largest exporter. This also compensated for the rather pathetic adherence of Mexico, which hitherto had not exported more than 100 tonnes to the EU except in the single, exceptional year of 1992. The USA and the other complainants had already initiated a case against the EU in the preceding year, but had aborted it and started again once Ecuador became a WTO member.

In November 1994, following the advice of the second GATT panel, the EU and ACP countries had jointly requested a waiver under Article XXV.5 of the GATT so that provisions of the Lomé Convention conferring preferences on the ACP would no longer be in breach of GATT. This was granted by consensus under the GATT and subsequently extended by the new WTO till the end of February 2000, when the Fourth Lomé Convention would expire. But the USA and Guatemala reserved their rights and a large part of the WTO case revolved around precisely what the terms of the waiver meant.

Finally, the Uruguay Round had settled the question of the legality of the Community's controversial tariff. Each contracting party to the Final Act listed specific commits in a schedule. The EU had included in this a tariff quota for bananas of 2.2 million tonnes at 75 ecus and an out-of quota tariff of 822 ecus per tonne in 1995 (722 ecus for the ACP), declining by equal instalments to 680 ecus on full implementation of the Uruguay Round commitments. Although Guatemala challenged these in the panel proceedings, the panel confirmed the validity of these tariff bindings in the Uruguay Round Schedule.

## The Rulings

The following sections outline the panel's conclusions on some of the main issues raised.

### Country allocations

The allocation of fixed percentages of the tariff quota to specific countries under the BFA stirred up a hornets' nest. Opponents of the BFA claimed that it discriminated against others and thereby contravened the GATT. The panel's ruling was more complex and more subtle. It ruled that the GATT permitted country-specific allocation of tariff quota shares to a substantial supplier, but only if shares were allocated to *all* other substantial suppliers. These were defined, on the basis of past GATT practice, as those accounting for 10 per cent or more of the market affected. Equally, if shares were allocated to any country 'not having a substantial interest', then they must be allocated to *all* others not having a substantial interest.

Two BFA countries, Colombia (16 per cent in 1989–91) and Costa Rica (20 per cent) were substantial suppliers and, at the time of the Agreement, were the only substantial suppliers who were GATT Members. Two others, Ecuador (15 per cent) and Panama (18 per cent) joined the GATT later. The panel pointed out that the existence of the BFA could not abrogate the rights of subsequent newcomers who were substantial suppliers. But the BFA was, in any event, ruled incompatible with the GATT (Article XIII) because it included two non-substantial suppliers, Nicaragua (1.7 per cent) and Venezuela (virtually 0 per cent) but not others.

This ruling had serious implications for ACP countries, and particularly for the Caribbean; these were the most vulnerable, since their individual country allocations were their guarantee of access. But all the ACP countries were non-substantial suppliers. By the logic of the BFA case, none should therefore have allocations unless allocations were made to all non-substantial suppliers, actual and potential, which simply would not be practicable to operate. Their one salvation was that the waiver for Lomé should exempt them from conformity with the rules on this.

**The waiver**

The key section of the waiver read:

> The provisions of paragraph 1 of Article I of the General Agreement shall be waived, until 29 February 2000, to the extent necessary to permit the European Communities to provide preferential treatment for products originating in ACP States as required by the relevant provisions of the Fourth Lomé Convention, without being required to extend the same preferential treatment to like products of any other contracting party.

This gave rise to two crucial questions. First, what was actually 'required by' the Lomé Convention? Second, since the waiver referred only to Article I of the GATT, which deals with tariff preferences, what were the implications for differential treatment in the administration of the tariff quota, which fell foul of Article XIII?

In answering the first question, the panel ominously insisted on their right to interpret the Convention for themselves, in a way that differed from that of the parties to the Convention.

The Community was committed under Protocol 5 of Lomé to ensure that 'no ACP State shall be placed, as regards access to its traditional markets and its advantages on those markets, in a less favourable situation than in the past or at present.' The panel concluded that the allocation of country-specific quotas was a reasonable way to transpose that obligation to a single market regime. But they also concluded that, since Lomé IV had been signed in December 1989 and applied from 1990, quotas should be limited to the highest volumes imported before 1991. This ruled out higher volumes that had been allocated to some countries to meet particular problems.

Even though the allocation of tariff quotas to traditional ACP suppliers was deemed to be required by Lomé, it was still inconsistent with Article XIII of the GATT. That article laid down strict rules for the administration of quotas, including tariff quotas. These prohibited any discrimination between members and required the allocation to reflect as closely as possible the pattern of distribution that might be expected to occur in the absence of quotas. This raised the problem that the waiver referred only to Article I, not to Article XIII.

The panel nevertheless concluded that Article XIII must be covered by implication:

> in our view, ... tariff preferences alone would not allow the EC to provide market access opportunities and advantages required of it by the Lomé Convention. In other words, in order to give real effect to the Lomé waiver, it needs to cover Article XIII to the extent necessary to allow the EC to allocate country-specific quotas shares to the ACP countries in the amount of their pre-1991 best-ever exports to the EC ... logically, we have no choice therefore but to interpret the waiver so that it accomplishes that objective.

This was a vital ruling for the ACP.

The panel also ruled that the waiver covered the tariff preferences extended to ACP countries that had not been traditional suppliers of bananas to the Community, since the Lomé Convention specifically provided for preferential treatment of ACP products (Lomé Article 168).

### Licence allocation

These were important reassurances for the Community. But the panel came down against most of the other controversial elements of the regime. The allocation of 30 per cent of the tariff quota to operators who had previously imported ACP or Community bananas was deemed to be in breach of the GATT. The panel did not consider that the cross-subsidisation that this provided was required by Lomé. Moreover, the system also protected EC producers and this too was in breach of the GATT (Article XIII.4).

Similarly the complex system of allocating licences according to different activity functions was deemed discriminatory because it was more burdensome than the arrangements applying to imports of traditional ACP bananas. This could not be justified as a requirement of Lomé since licensing advantages were not among the benefits traditionally enjoyed by traditional ACP suppliers.

The panel also upheld complaints against the system of 'hurricane licences', which enabled traders to import dollar fruit specifically to replace crops in the Caribbean or other ACP or EU origins destroyed by hurricane. The panel ruled that this provided an incentive to purchase bananas of EU or ACP origin rather than from other third countries.

### Trade in Services (GATS)

The panel made a landmark judgment in ruling that the EU licensing procedures for bananas contravened the provisions not only of the GATT, which deals with imports of goods, but also of the new GATS, which covered trade in services. The panel took the view that services covered every aspect of distributing bananas, and that the licensing procedures that breached the non-discrimination rules of the GATT similarly breached those of the GATS. This surprised many trade experts. The EU had indeed argued that the GATT and the GATS were mutually exclusive, a view which the panel strongly rejected. The implications of this ruling will extend far beyond bananas.

*Banana Wars*

The principle of the GATS is identical to the GATT in banning rules against any form of discrimination against a contracting party, but the perceived basis for discrimination was sometimes subtly different on specific issues. Thus on hurricane licences the argument was that these licences were issued exclusively to operators who represented ACP or EU producers. Since in practice these were mainly EU operators, this effectively discriminated against third-country operators.

## Effect of Rulings

This panel's mandatory ruling would necessitate radical changes to the Community regime. For the ACP it entailed the loss of the cross-subsidisation made possible by the B quota system. Without this, they might not be able to secure a viable return for their higher-cost bananas. The only safeguards left intact for the ACP, apart from the existence of the tariff quotas, were the modest tariff preferences and the country quota allocations for the traditional ACP, both of which were deemed to be protected by the Lomé waiver. However, even this degree of comfort was not to last.

## The Appeal

The Community decided to appeal against a number of aspects of the panel ruling, including the ruling on the GATS aspects. Whereas the panel is made up of three trade experts, who are advised by the permanent WTO staff, the appeal body comprises three jurists. The appeal upheld nearly all the panel's decisions, including its interpretation of the GATS. But it reversed the crucial panel decision that the waiver must be deemed to cover Article XIII as well as Article I and thus permit allocation of quota to traditional ACP supplying countries. The appeal panel ruled that waivers need to be interpreted strictly and that it must therefore be assumed that, had the Council wished the waiver to cover Article XIII, it would have said so in the terms of the waiver. The common-sense approach of the panel was overridden by the rigid letter of the law.

This was a severe blow to the Community and even more so to the ACP. It was a ruling that would greatly impede subsequent Community efforts to meet its obligations to the ACP in a manner compatible with the GATT.

The presiding jurist had been an American. It is commonly accepted that jurists are immune to national bias and must operate on the taxi rank system, taking cases by turns. But his appointment did not suggest great sensitivity on the part of the WTO, when the USA was a leading protagonist, and this factor added to the unease among ACP countries over the stringency of the ruling.

## Treatment of ACP Countries

Moreover, the ACP countries had felt very shabbily treated by the original panel, and this made it difficult for them to accept the outcome with equanimity. It was the ACP countries that had most at stake in these proceedings, because they stood to lose their entire banana trade. For some ACP states, such as the Windward Islands, this trade was a matter of economic life or death. Yet the WTO regarded the dispute as exclusively between the USA and the four Latin American complainants on one side and the European Community on the other. The ACP were accorded only third-party status, and were thus placed in the same category as countries like Japan, which do not export bananas, but might have an interest in the wider implications of the case.

This meant that the ACP countries were seriously handicapped in their attempts to present their case. They were not allowed to attend the organisational meetings, which decided on issues affecting the conduct of the case; they were allowed to attend only selected sessions and to make a 'brief statement'. They were denied the right to pose questions to the Complainants or the EU on factual and legal matters or to submit rebuttals to their submissions. Moreover, they did not receive copies of the panel's report when it was sent to the complainants and the European Community for vetting, but only after it had been published.

Worst of all, the panel chairman, at the request of the complainants, ejected from the sessions the two private lawyers advising the

Windward Islands delegations. These lawyers had been formally
accredited in writing by the Windward Island governments as
members of their delegations. But at the organisational meeting,
to which third parties were not admitted, it had been intimated
that only members of government would be present at panel
meetings. This was interpreted as meaning permanent government
employees. So the four Windward Islands were left without legal
advice during these crucial sessions, facing the serried ranks of
permanent legal advisers to the USA and other complainants.

Two main justifications were offered for this extraordinary
action. One was that private lawyers could not be trusted to maintain confidentiality in the same way as civil servants; the other
was that the practice of bringing private lawyers 'would entail
disproportionately large financial burdens' for smaller countries.
The implication that it is more economic to employ full-time
permanent legal experts on the GATT rather than to hire them
on the very rare occasions that they are needed is hard to follow.
To add insult to injury, the chairman subsequently rebuked the
delegations concerned for breach of confidentiality when the story
of the ejection appeared in the press.

It is an interesting reflection of the atmosphere of this case that
the complainants should have pressed for this exclusion. The move
may have been influenced by the fact that one of the private legal
advisers had formerly been a senior member of the staff of the
USTR. There may have been some resentment over what looked
like gamekeeper turned poacher. But it was very petty. On nearly
all procedural issues, the chairman, and presumably his advisers,
took the line that there could be no flexibility in applying the
rules, or even conventions, unless the complainants agreed.

When the case went for appeal the unjust decision on attendance
of private lawyers was overturned and they were freely admitted.
But by then the damage had been done.

# 14

## A Disputed Conformity

The arbitration panel reported in September 1997 and the Community asked to be given until 1 January 1999 to bring their regime into conformity with the ruling. The complainants opposed this timetable, pressing for implementation by 1 July 1998. The issue had to go to arbitration under the Disputes Settlement Procedure. The arbitrator endorsed the Community claim that 1 January 1999 met the requirement for conformity within a 'reasonable period of time', particularly in view of the complexity of the EU legislation process, involving fifteen member states and the European Parliament. But the need to go to arbitration on such an issue was indicative of the attitudes aroused by this dispute. Every point in the process had to be fought out to the end. Nevertheless, in February 1998, the USTR formally terminated its proceedings under section 301 of the US Trade Act in the light of the EU's undertaking, in December 1997, to implement the WTO rulings by 1 January 1999.

### The Amended Regime

For the EU, finding a way to conform was not easy. The Community still had its Treaty commitments to the ACP but the WTO ruling greatly reduced its ability to fulfil them. Both the USA and several member states, led by Germany and Sweden, argued that the Community should now sweep away the protective regime and opt for a single tariff with no quantitative restrictions

Fortuitously, the UK again held the presidency of the Community in the first half of 1998, which proved the decisive period, and again played a pivotal role in securing a settlement. There had been some shift in the political balance since the first regime was agreed at the end of 1992. None of the new states that joined the Community in 1995, Sweden, Austria and Finland, had historic ties with ACP countries and all favoured a more liberal regime. Indeed the Swedish Minister of Agriculture had declared publicly, before Sweden's accession, her intention to work with other like-minded states to sweep away the restrictive banana regime.

Moreover, the new states, as well as Denmark, felt that the regime operated unfairly against them because import licences, through which the dollar quota was shared out, were awarded mainly to primary importers – that is, those importing directly from the country of origin. But because the volume of their imports was relatively small, traders in these states bought their bananas from the major shippers like Chiquita. They were, therefore, secondary importers and so received licences on only a small proportion of their previously traded volumes. This affected the price they had to pay and thus their profits, even though the volumes imported might remain the same. The resentment felt by traders in these countries was a more potent factor affecting their governments than more general principles of free trade. But it meant that there was now a majority of member states by number that favoured a more liberal system.

However, apart from Germany, these were all relatively small states in terms of population and therefore commanded fewer votes in the Council. They did not have the qualified majority necessary to get legislation through the Council. Nor did those, led by the UK and France, which were committed to retaining a restricted market for the benefit of the ACP and Community growers. Each group constituted a blocking minority.

The responsibility for submitting proposals for a revised regime rested on the Commission. Because the Community still had to fulfil the Lomé commitment to the ACP and to safeguard Community growers, the Commission tried to salvage as much of the existing regime as it could from the WTO ruling.

Yet vital elements of the old regime had to be scrapped. In the light of the ruling, it would no longer be possible to cross-subsidise ACP and EU bananas through the B licence system (which allocated 30 per cent of the dollar quota to those that had imported Community or ACP bananas). Nor could the ACP countries now be allocated specific-country quotas, as in the past, to guarantee them access for specified volumes. These were severe limitations, particularly for the traditional Caribbean exporting states, which were the most vulnerable ACP countries.

The Commission proposal was therefore to retain the existing tariff quotas for dollar bananas, amounting to 2,553 million tonnes, that had obtained since the accession of the three new member states (Sweden, Finland and Austria) in 1995. The tariff would also remain at 75 ecus. The proposal also provided for the allocation of specific quota shares to each of the four countries that qualified in WTO terms as substantial suppliers – Ecuador, Costa Rica, Colombia and Panama. This accounted for over 90 per cent of the dollar quota. For the ACP there was to be a single, collective, tariff quota providing duty-free entry for 857,000 tonnes of ACP bananas, replacing the individual country allocations.

The Commission proposal had been cleared with its own legal service as compatible with the WTO ruling, but Germany and several other member states remained sceptical. They therefore insisted that the Council of Ministers obtain independent advice from the Council's own lawyers. However, the Council lawyers, treading delicately, did not advise against the proposals, although they stressed that only the WTO itself could give a definitive view on compatibility.

The lack of any negative comment from the lawyers took much of the heart out of the opposition. Another relevant factor was the more relaxed view of sections of the trade in Germany and elsewhere, since it was recognised that the quota system could yield some benefits in the form of better prices and would be less objectionable with the removal of its most controversial features following the panel ruling.

After long discussion among member states, the proposals were finally put to a vote in the Council at its last meeting under the UK presidency, in June 1998. In order to maximise the chances of getting the necessary qualified majority, the presidency again resorted, as in 1992, to including the proposals on bananas in a package containing other agricultural issues important to different member states. Members could, in principle, vote against specific items in the package, including bananas, while supporting the others, but, in the event, only Denmark and the Netherlands voted against. Even Germany supported the proposal when it came to the crunch (in contrast to 1992), as did Sweden. This may have reflected recognition that there was no real alternative consistent with the EU's commitments or capable of commanding the necessary majority. The formal legislation was adopted in July 1998 to come into effect on 1 January 1999.

This revised regime left the ACP countries with much less market support than in the past. Moreover, replacing the country allocations by a single quota for all ACP countries significantly reduced the protection for the more vulnerable, because it opened the way for lower-cost ACP countries to take a greater share of that quota to the detriment of the less competitive.

By way of compensation for lower protection, the settlement included a ten-year programme of aid to enable ACP suppliers 'to adapt to new market conditions and improve competitiveness'. But the aid package gave no direct or immediate help to growers, since it would be granted only for specific programmes and projects to be approved by the European Commission. This could take some years and would do nothing to keep growers in business meanwhile if prices were allowed to collapse. But the combination of a continued, though less supportive, quota regime and a potential aid programme at least offered the prospect of time and means to adapt.

## USA and Ecuador Challenge Again

The Community had rejected a US request, following the WTO rulings, to explore mutually agreeable solutions: and however unsatisfactory the revised regime may have seemed to the ACP, it definitely did not satisfy the USA or Ecuador. The USA insisted that a separate tariff quota for the ACP was discriminatory and that adequate protection could be given to the ACP and to the Caribbean in particular, in other ways (see Chapter 15).

Both countries complained to the WTO's Disputes Settlement Board that the amended regime still failed to conform to the rulings. Subsequent consultations with the EU under the disputes settlements procedure failed to lead to any agreement. In November 1998, the USA therefore gave notice of its intention to apply sanctions unilaterally on Community trade for what they regarded as non-compliance with the WTO ruling. The USA did not consider it necessary to secure confirmation by the WTO that the EU remained in breach of the rulings. In its view, that was self-evident and it was not prepared to contemplate a continuing succession of adverse rulings against the EU which, as the USA saw it, the EU would then purport to remedy, after another long delay, by a different set of illegal measures, in a potentially unending cycle.

As a result, implementation of the new regime on 1 January 1999 led immediately to three separate initiatives in the WTO:

1. The USA sought WTO authority to impose sanctions, in the form of punitive tariffs, on selected Community products up to a total value of $520 million. The USA did not wait for the panel ruling before taking punitive action. Although it did not formally impose the additional duties until the panel reported, the US required importers of the target goods from the EU to deposit a bond for the amount of the additional duty from 3 March 1999. This had the same effect as applying the sanctions immediately. The EU sought arbitration on those sanctions.
2. Ecuador requested the reappointment of the previous panel to determine that the new regime failed to conform to WTO rules. This was the more orthodox approach, which the USA disdained.
3. The EU sought positive confirmation from the WTO that their new regime did conform to the panel ruling.

The WTO reappointed the same panel that had taken the case in 1997 to rule on each of these separate but interrelated claims.

## Second WTO Ruling

The panel reported in April. It confirmed that the regime did not comply with the ruling and that the USA was entitled to apply sanctions. But it calculated the damage to US trade, and consequently the legitimate amount for the sanctions, at $191 million a year rather than the $520 million that the USA had already begun imposing. The panel reached this conclusion by comparing the impact of the regime on US trade compared with that of a hypothetical alternative regime that would have conformed to the ruling.

Ecuador had taken the more appropriate course of challenging the new regime in the WTO. Ecuador's principal, and most vulnerable, target was the separate global quota for the ACP. The Community had taken the view that, since the WTO had ruled out country allocations for individual ACP suppliers, as they were all non-substantial suppliers, there was no other way of ring-fencing the ACP from Latin American competition than to have a separate volume set aside for them to share.

This panel found the global provision for the ACP to be contrary to the rules of non-discrimination on a number of grounds. The panel had previously ruled that the Lomé Convention justified allocations of quota only up to each country's best pre-1991 performance. But a single ACP quota would not preclude a country from exceeding that level and therefore receiving benefits greater than the panel deemed to be justified by Lomé. More important, in 1997 the appellate body, overturning the finding of the panel, had ruled that the Lomé waiver did not cover Article XIII, which precludes discrimination in the administration of quotas. The Community was therefore bound to apply the quotas in a way which did not discriminate between GATT parties and which reflected as closely as possible the distribution of trade that would occur without quotas. The panel concluded that a separate quota of 857,000 tonnes reserved for the ACP failed to do this.

The panel also ruled that licences allocated to operators on the basis of performance in 1994–96 were discriminatory, because the pattern of trade in that period reflected some residual element of the B licence system, the activity functions and other factors, which the panel had previously ruled to be discriminatory.

Perhaps the most telling comment of the panel came in response to Ecuador's objection to the specific quota allocation to substantial suppliers, since these could limit Ecuador's potential for expansion. The panel found these allocations discriminatory because they were based on the reference period 1994–96, which was a period when the regime in operation had been ruled to be incompatible with WTO rules. Since the same objection applied to the preceding national regimes, the panel concluded that country-specific allocations could not be imposed on the basis of trade in any past period, but could only be made by agreement with all the parties. It was this ruling that would subsequently provoke a two-year search for agreement on a base period for allocating quotas and push the Community towards the desperate expedient of allocating them instead on a 'first come, first served' basis.

## Panel Advice on Compliance

Ecuador had astutely requested the panel to indicate what type of regime it would regard as WTO-compatible. The panel agreed to do this since one attempt at implementation 'has proven to be at least partly unsuccessful'. The panel's advice was depressingly illuminating. Any form of separate tariff quota for the ACP would require a specific waiver from the application of Article XIII. This was regarded as a serious obstacle. Only one waiver had ever been given before for Article XIII and the voting requirement of 75 per cent support meant that in practice this could only be secured in agreement with the USA and the Latin Americans.

Another possibility cited was a tariff-only regime, that is to say a regime that provided no other protection to the ACP except a tariff. But if there were to be a tariff preference for the ACP, such as duty-free entry, this would also require a waiver (from Article I). Moreover, the bound tariff of 75 ecus would not by itself provide adequate protection for the ACP, and any higher level of tariff would have to be negotiated in the WTO.

Thus the WTO proceedings left the Community in a double bind. The ruling made it almost impossible to find GATT-compatible means of honouring its obligations to the ACP. But until it introduced a regime that implemented the panel's findings, member states would continue to suffer the economic and political consequences of the trade sanctions that the USA was imposing with full WTO authority on selected EU exports to the USA.

## US Sanctions

US sanctions had been deliberately pitched to cause most pain to
those member states that were most supportive of the Community
regime. Thus, notwithstanding the 'special relationship', including
the joint US and UK air patrols over Iraq, the UK was singled
out for the heaviest sanctions while Denmark and the Netherlands,
who had voted against the regime, faced none. The most serious
threat to the UK was inclusion of Scottish cashmere products
in the original target list. The industry was situated in politically
sensitive territory, which also happened to include the constituency
of a minister in the Department of Trade. The industry claimed
that the sanctions would place 2,400 jobs at risk. To avert this, the
government rapidly undertook to meet the costs of the additional
charges. When the arbitration panel ruled in April that the USA
was entitled to only $191 million of compensation, rather than the
$520 that they were taking, cashmere was taken off the list, no
doubt in response to heavy pressure from the UK government.

The USA had already given formal notice on 10 November
1998 of its intention to impose sanctions on specified products
from 3 March 1999 if Community restrictions on imports of
Latin American bananas were not removed. For the benefit of US
businesses, the Office of the United States Trade Representative
(USTR) published in the Federal register a list of forty-two target
products on which it invited comments, as it was statutorily required to do. This led to a massive lobbying campaign by importing
US companies that might be affected. As a result of this pressure,
many items were dropped from the list. Many more had to be
dropped from the list when the arbitration ruling reduced the
value of permitted sanctions to little more than one-third of the
original target. The final list published in April 1999 contained
only nine types of product: handbags (particularly affecting France)
peccorino cheese (Italy), electric coffee makers, felt paper and
paperboard, folding cartons, boxes and cases, bath preparations,
industrial batteries and bed linens.

To some extent sanctions proved a double-edged sword, since
they damaged some US firms that were too small to be avid
readers of the Federal Register or to afford to employ high-powered

lobbyists in Washington. These consequently found out too late that imports vital to their business were being priced out of the market. As *Time* magazine commented: 'When a fruit baron wanted to conquer more of the European market, he got Washington to launch a trade war for him. The victims of the cross fire? A bunch of ordinary Americans who never saw it coming.'[1]

A forlorn attempt was made to get through Congress legislation to exempt small US businesses from these sanctions,[2] but it had no chance. More remarkable was the success of supporters of Chiquita in securing legislation designed to reinforce the sanctions. They secured a provision that made it mandatory on the US trade representative to rotate the sanctions among different products unless the company that had triggered the action, namely Chiquita, agreed that it was not necessary to do so. Such a 'carousel' would increase both the political and the economic impact of the sanctions. This requirement was secured by a form of legislative sleight of hand. It was added to the report stage of legislation on a completely different issue, the Africa Growth and Opportunity Act, just before that report was presented for a vote, so that members of Congress had no opportunity to vote separately on the carousel provision. In the event, the administration managed to avoid applying the 'carousel' provision.

Even more remarkable was an attempt to secure legislation that would have prevented sanctions from being lifted without the agreement of Chiquita. This would have given Chiquita a veto on any settlement. The desire to secure the removal of the sanctions was an ever-present, though by no means dominant, factor during the long search for an acceptable means of complying with the WTO ruling.

The WTO had also granted Ecuador the right to impose sanctions, but in the event Ecuador refrained from imposing them. This seems to have been largely because to do so would have harmed Ecuador's own economy as much as that of the EU.

The Community subsequently challenged in the WTO the provision in the 1974 US Trade Act which enabled the USA to impose sanctions before the WTO had ruled on the issue in question. Eleven other countries, including Japan and Canada, supported the Community case. The WTO panel ruled that such action was incompatible with WTO rules and that Section 301 could only be considered to conform if the USA undertook in future to act always in accordance with WTO procedures in its use of discretionary powers under Section 301. The USA gave that undertaking.

# 15

## *Spin and Reality*

Parallel with the legal battles over the compatibility of the Community regime with international and US laws, a separate public-relations battle was being waged by academics, politicians and public-relations experts. All accepted as the point of departure that the Caribbean states, more than any others, presented a special problem, because they were so heavily dependent on banana exports yet could not compete without some form of market support. But many argued strongly that the Community regime was not an economic, appropriate or just way of resolving this problem. This chapter considers some of the arguments deployed on both sides of the dispute.

### Aid versus Trade

One of the most persistent and ferocious critics of the regime was an economist, Brent Borrell. He published a series of 'Bananarama' reports, starting in 1992 with a research paper for the World Bank, which carried the customary Bank disclaimer of responsibility for the views therein. Borrell argued strongly in favour of making direct aid payments to ACP exporting countries rather than protecting their banana exports through a managed market. Following the Community's adoption of the tariff quota regime, Borrell produced further editions of Bananarama lambasting that decision. A 1996 version claimed that the regime imposed a total of $2 billion a year in higher costs on Community consumers, yet passed on only $0.15 billion to the ACP:

That is, it costs consumers $13.25 to transfer $1.0 of aid. Worse still, for every dollar of aid reaching its target it causes collateral damage to other developing countries which export bananas. This occurs because price and export opportunities are lessened. The net benefit to developing countries is therefore zero.[1]

This provocative claim was strongly criticised by other economists. These maintained that the economic model that Borrell used for the calculations was flawed; that his results depended on the use of questionable assumptions; and that it was wrong to base the calculations on prices in the year 1991/92, when the price of dollar bananas was the lowest for twenty years due to heavy oversupply.[2]

The director of agricultural economics at the University of Exeter, also a consultant to the World Bank, concluded that the models used were 'an inadequate representation of the "real world" market place' and that 'The calculated losses and gains attributed to the new Banana regime are inaccurate, and cannot be taken as a reasonable estimate of the economic impact of the new regime.'[3]

Nevertheless, the press across Europe unquestioningly lapped up Bananarama, particularly where it fitted into a paper's free-trade philosophy. Borrell, then chief market economist at the Centre for Economic Studies in Canberra, received World Bank funding for Bananarama III, which the press then heralded as a World Bank pronouncement. Even the prestigious and influential *Financial Times* placed an uncritical summary under a page-wide headline 'EU banana policy "perverse and inefficient" says World Bank'.[4] What hope, then, for an informed view from lesser fry!

Yet the fact that Borrell's Bananarama arguments may have been based on dubious and misleading statistics does not necessarily invalidate his main thesis, namely that direct aid payments would have been a more effective means of helping the Caribbean and other ACP countries and much less disruptive of international trade. This is the essential debate of trade versus aid.

Borrell seemed to regard the EU banana regime solely as an inefficient vehicle for transferring given sums of money to the ACP. He complained that it was wasteful because it not only imposed unnecessary costs on consumers but also required the

ACP countries concerned 'to use up and pay for resources to grow bananas in order to qualify for the aid'.[5] He saw aid not as a means of sustaining growers in business but as a means of inducing those that could not be competitive to quit the industry and leave the field to those who could supply consumers at a lower cost.

This may have been the ideal solution for an academic economist but it was not feasible in the real world of 1993. The EU had a Treaty commitment to maintain the ACP banana trade and the pre-existing benefits of traditional ACP exporting countries on the EU market until the year 2000. To replace these benefits by aid aimed at closing down the ACP banana industries was simply not an option for the EU.

In addition to this Treaty constraint, the economic, social and political importance of the banana industry to the ACP countries concerned would have made such a policy untenable. This was the case, above all, for the Windward Islands in the Caribbean. At that time, the banana export trade to the EU provided the largest source of all export earnings on three of the four main islands – as much as 70 per cent in Dominica – and over one-third of all employment.

Moreover, the trade ensured a weekly shipping service to the UK that was vital to the life of the islands: only bananas could provide the volume to make this regular service economic. These exports provided the livelihood for well over 20,000 households, and purchases by these households, ranging from cartons for the bananas to food and clothes for the growers and their families, provided a vital stimulus for the rest of the economy.

### Deficiency Payment Alternative

There was, theoretically, an alternative means of maintaining the ACP industries, at least for a transitional period, together with the free-market regime that Borrell and others wanted. In 1992, Borrell had suggested a deficiency payments system for ACP growers as a second-best option. He proposed that the EU provide unrestricted access for banana imports from all sources, while safeguarding

ACP growers by means of a system of direct payments, making up the difference between the market price they received and the amount that they needed. He argued that this would benefit both EU consumers and Latin American producers and could be financed out of a 20 per cent tariff on all imports, including those from the ACP, which were currently exempt.[6]

Such an approach would undoubtedly have attractions for growers, provided that the target price provided a viable return, and also to consumers, because it implied lower prices than under a quota system. The taxpayers would bear the strain. But the Lomé Convention precluded imposing a tariff on ACP imports. Moreover, the existing tariff formed an integral part of the EU budget, so that in practice new resources would have to be found to replace this income if the proceeds were to be diverted instead to subsidising ACP imports. Given the controversial nature of Borrell's economic model, the cost could turn out to be a lot greater than his estimate. No government could be expected to take on such an open-ended financial commitment even to their own growers, let alone for third-country growers as well.

Deficiency payments tend to be extremely costly unless imports of competing products are restricted. Before it joined the Community, the UK used to support its farmers by means of a deficiency payments system, unsupported by import quotas, for major commodities such as milk, meat and cereals and found this increasingly costly to sustain. Primary producers the world over took advantage of this relatively rare free access, with the result that prices fell and the cost of deficiency payments spiralled well beyond the estimates agreed by Parliament. From the early 1960s the government was driven increasingly to negotiating deals with supplying countries designed to restrict imports on a voluntarily agreed basis. Conviction that this system was not tenable in the long term contributed to the mass of argument in favour of the UK joining the Community.

The EU banana regime did provide for deficiency payments to be made to its own banana growers to bring their average returns up to a specified reference price. But this was possible only because that regime restricted imports of the cheaper Latin American bananas through a tariff quota and thus limited the cost of aid payments. Without a tariff quota system to maintain stability in the market, the cost of maintaining those deficiency payments could have proved unsustainable. *The quota regime was therefore at least as essential to maintaining the EU's commitment to its own producers as it was to fulfilling its obligations to the ACP.* But the member states of the Community were never prepared to entertain the idea of extending these payments, or any comparable form of subsidy, to the ACP. No doubt this was considered far too expensive and far too dangerous a precedent.

## The Doctrine of Comparative Advantage

At the root of the drive for free trade is the economic doctrine of comparative advantage. This maintains that if each country concentrates on producing goods or services in which it has the greatest relative efficiency, then the sum total of wealth is maximised all round. There is no doubt that the Latin Americans are best at producing bananas for export, because they have an absolute advantage in vast areas of flat land, fertile soils, a suitable climate, pools of cheap labour and reasonable proximity to the main markets.

Banana production is also what some Caribbean countries do best, notably the Windward Islands, even though they cannot compete on price with Latin America, for reasons already explained. There is no other product, apart from tourism, in which the Windward Islands would be more competitive and no alternative product could replace the earnings and employment that bananas provide. Much effort and investment has been devoted over many years to seeking alternative export crops. But there is none which can be grown in the Windward Islands that could not be produced more competitively in tropical Latin America where land and soil conditions are far superior. The handicaps of size, terrain and climate, which apply to bananas, would apply equally to any other agricultural export crop.

The smallness of the population, averaging around 100,000 per island, provides no significant domestic market for any alternative enterprises. The one other comparable source of earnings and employment is tourism, but there is a limit to which this can be developed on small islands without becoming self-defeating, by reducing the environmental attractions on which the trade has been built.

Moreover, tourism depends on a reasonably tranquil social and political environment. Loss of the banana trade, which provides around half of all earnings and more than a third of employment, would place that social and political stability at risk, with adverse consequences for the tourist trade.

There are strong arguments for restructuring and improving the banana industry in the islands and elsewhere in the Caribbean to provide the maximum possible chance of the industry surviving in the tougher, more competitive, circumstances demanded by trade liberalisation. This is considered more fully in Chapter 20. But the economies of the islands will continue to depend on retaining a viable banana export trade and with it the vital weekly shipping service that only the bulk export volumes of bananas can justify.

## The US Scene

### The Congressional Black Caucus

In Washington, there was a small but effective lobby that pressed the Caribbean cause. This was led by Democratic Representative Maxine Waters of California, a black American once irreverently described as 'the personification of spunk'. She was one of thirteen children reared by a single mother and began work at the age of 13 in factories and segregated restaurants. After serving for fourteen years in the California Assembly, she was elected to the US Congress in 1990, and in 1997/8 she was chair of the 39-member Congressional Black Caucus.

Maxine Waters worked tirelessly and courageously on behalf of the Caribbean banana growers. She was supported by the group TransAfrica, led by Randall Robinson, which aimed to promote economic development and political stability in Africa and the Caribbean. In a series of letters to the President and to the US trade representative over the period of the dispute and in public statements in Congress and elsewhere, Maxine Waters and her supporters pursued two main themes. The first was moral, the second that of enlightened US self-interest.

The moral argument was that 'the tiny island democracies of the Caribbean' should not be made to suffer as a result of a trade stand-off between the USA and the EU, undertaken at the behest of a single US company for a commodity which the USA did not even export. The US action was likely to deny these islands the urgently needed revenues with which to manage their economies and to erode the social cohesion for which the islands were known.

The argument of self-interest was that the destruction of the Caribbean banana industry would simply force growers into the arms of the drug traffickers. Already in March 1996, an International Narcotics Control Strategy Report by the US State Department stated that the terrain in St Vincent, in the Windward Islands, was most attractive to South Americans transshipping cocaine and that struggling banana farmers had been turning to marijuana as a cash crop to replace lost earnings. Moreover, in June 1996, General John Sheehan, then Commander-in-Chief of the US Atlantic Command, publicly expressed his fear of regional destabilisation and increased drug flows if US policy on bananas did not change.

In 1996 Maxine Waters led an Eminent Persons Group, comprising members of Congress, academics, labour leaders and representatives of civic groups, on a visit to Jamaica and the Windward Islands, to see the problems at first hand. The Group published a report on the visit under the title 'Not Just a Trade Issue: Jeopardising Democracy and US National Interest in the Caribbean'. This stressed the dependence of the Caribbean on the banana trade and the severe economic and social consequences of the loss of that trade for these small, friendly democratic states. Destroying these economies would create social and political unrest on the USA's own doorstep, bringing the risk of illegal immigration and above all drug trafficking. Geographically, Jamaica and the Windward Islands were sandwiched between the world's largest producer and the world's largest consumer of drugs.

*Newsweek* magazine took up similar themes in its cover story on 28 April 1997, when news of the adverse WTO ruling first broke. The front-page subtitle set the tone: 'Chiquita vs the Caribbean: Island Economies May Be New Victims of Free Trade'. The article contrasted US policy then with the US attitude to the Caribbean during the Cold War: 'The United States would not have permitted, much less authored, such a blow to the Caribbean back in the 1980s.'

## USTR viewpoint

The office of the United States Trade Representative (USTR) was both more hard-nosed and more pragmatic. It too accepted that the Caribbean constituted a special case and was prepared to agree to special measures being taken to help them. But the Caribbean accounted for less than 9 per cent of the EU market and USTR argued that it was neither right nor necessary to impose a restrictive and discriminatory market regime that impeded US trade solely for the purpose of safeguarding that small part of it. USTR argued that the needs of other ACP countries could be met through a tariff preference, while the Community could meet the special needs of the Caribbean by means of a system of deficiency payments or 'negative tariffs'.

For the Community this was a non-starter. It would not have been politically feasible for them to differentiate between ACP countries in that way and they were opposed to deficiency payments to third-country growers on grounds of precedent and cost. Above all, they needed a tariff quota system, in any event, to limit the cost of support for their own producers. Moreover, as the first GATT case had confirmed (see Chapter 10), tariff quotas were acceptable under WTO rules, provided that they were not applied in a discriminatory way. So battle was joined on that issue.

Leading Republicans in Congress urged the President to take a tough line. They were supported by the Farm Bureau and the meat industry, which were incensed by the European Community's ban on imports of beef treated with hormones. The Bureau teamed up with Chiquita to place full-page advertisements in the *Washington Post* and other national newspapers with the telling slogan 'If its going to have any teeth, the World Trade Organisation has to cut them on beef and bananas.' That also succinctly encapsulated the view of the administration.

## The sleaze factor

An interesting feature was the extent to which the press and others saw the US action as an example of undue influence bought by money – what in the UK would be called the sleaze factor. In *Time* magazine of 7 February 2000 the cover story, headed 'How to Become a Top Banana', spells out in detail the influence that was brought to bear:

> Europe first offended Lindner [who controlled Chiquita] when it imposed import restrictions on bananas from Latin America, where his plantations are located. Lindner then contributed a quarter of a million dollars to the Democrats. Gore [then vice-president] called and asked for more. Lindner gave it. And then some more. So much more that Lindner had dinner in the White House, attended a coffee klatch there for the truly generous and slept in the Lincoln Bedroom. Along the way, he periodically met with the then US Trade Representative Mickey Kantor and his staff, the officials who ultimately sought the trade sanctions intended to punish the Europeans and force them to give Lindner what he wanted.

Lindner/Chiquita continued throughout the dispute to exercise an extraordinary influence through friends in Congress. One example was the unsuccessful attempt, cited in Chapter 12, to impose draconian penalties on countries adhering to the Banana Framework Agreement. Others, cited in the preceding chapter, related to the administration of trade sanctions against the EU, including the successful attempt to require sanctions to be rotated unless Chiquita agreed that this was not necessary; and the unsuccessful attempt to give Chiquita a veto on any settlement of the dispute.

## The *Cincinnati Enquirer*

One curious but troubling incident in this public-relations saga was the affair of the *Cincinnati Enquirer*. Cincinnati is the home of Chiquita Brands. Two reporters on the newspaper undertook a two-year study of Chiquita operations, which was encapsulated in an eighteen-page supplement published on 3 May 1998. This contained numerous articles impugning the company's business practices, including the manner in which it claimed Chiquita wielded political influence at home and abroad to the detriment of, among others, Caribbean banana growers.

Yet it transpired that these articles had been based partly on illegally obtained tapes of internal voice-mail messages within the company offices. When this was discovered, the *Enquirer* sacked the lead reporter, published a full apology and disclaimer on its front page in three successive weeks, and paid $10 million in compensation to Chiquita. The reporter ended up in prison. The fate of the journalist, and the fact that his source in the company was revealed, inspired a lot of copy, but none which ventured an opinion on whether the articles would have been justified if the material had been obtained legally.

## *Seeking an Agreed Solution*

The panel ruling on the Community's revised regime was delivered on 12 April 1999. The Community decided not to appeal against it (the precedent of 1997 was not encouraging). The Community therefore faced, once again, the need to conform to a WTO ruling on the banana regime. In a striking reversal of previous policy, the European Commission now sought from the outset to find a basis of agreement with all other interested parties and above all with the USA.

### Consultations with Major Parties

The consultations for this purpose revealed a widespread prefer-ence for maintaining some form of tariff quota system, at least for a transitional period. This was favoured by all the Latin American exporting countries, by Chiquita and by the ACP and was also acceptable to the US government. It was seen as a means of maintaining a remunerative market in Europe as well as meeting Community obligations to the ACP.

However, serious differences emerged over key elements of any new tariff quota regime, particularly the reference period for the allocation of the quota, which would largely determine market share. Ecuador, whose exports to the EU had increased in recent years, wanted the most recent period possible. But the USA and the Latin Americans other than Ecuador insisted on a period before the first regime was introduced in 1993. The Commission maintained that this was impossible for both legal and technical reasons. Using such a distant date would expose the Community to legal action in the European Court of Justice by companies penalised by it; and, in any event, records for that period were not adequate.

The ACP were anxious to maintain a separate ACP quota and they urged the Community to seek the necessary Article XIII waiver for this, but from soundings made with other parties the Commission concluded that this was simply not negotiable.

## Initial Commission Proposals

The Commission submitted a report on its consultations to the Council of Ministers in November 1999. This proposed a two-stage solution: a tariff quota regime till the end of 2005, then from 2006 a tariff-only system – no quotas, only a single, flat-rate tariff at a level to be negotiated. For the Commission was adamant that no permanent solution was possible without commitment from the outset to a firm date for ending the quota system.

In the first stage, the two existing tariff quotas intended primarily for dollar supplies (A/B), amounting to 2.553 million tonnes, would be retained at 75 euros duty, with duty-free entry for the ACP. Allocation would be on the basis of a historical reference period, if such a period could be agreed in further discussions. But failing that, the Commission proposed to administer the quota on the basis of 'first come, first served'. That meant no reference period, no prior allocation of quota shares, just a refined form of boat race. The Commission believed that this system was indisputably compatible with the GATT and was therefore a safe option of last resort.

A third quota of 850,000 tonnes would be open to all comers but with a tariff preference for the ACP of 275 euros. This was intended to replace the existing ACP quota that had been ruled to be against WTO rules. It would operate by a form of auction known as the strike price system, under which operators bid by offering a rate of duty that they would be prepared to pay to import a certain quantity of bananas. The rate of duty finally set would be at the level of the lowest bid necessary to bring in the total volume allocated for that auction (see Figure 16.1).

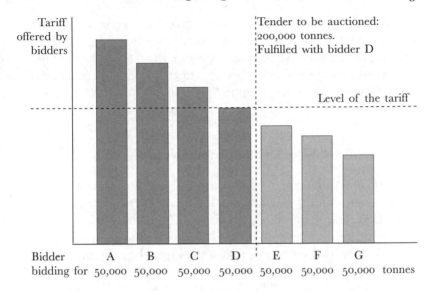

Assuming that a tender was for 200,000 tonnes and the bids came as illustrated. Then, as bids A + B + C + D = 200,000 tonnes, these bids are accepted and bids E, F, G are rejected. The tariff is set at the lowest level offered by the accepted bids (D). (*Source*: European Commission.)

**Figure 16.1** Striking price auctioning system

These proposals caused consternation, particularly among the ACP, but also among Latin American supplying countries, except Ecuador, and to Chiquita in the USA. The ACP believed that it would not be possible for them, and particularly for the smaller and more vulnerable among them, to maintain their trade on the basis of an auction system, even with a 275 euros preference. An auction system could not provide the certainty of access essential for rational and economic planning of shipping and other commercial contracts, which were normally made a year in advance.

Moreover, combining an auction system for the quota intended primarily for the ACP with a first-come, first-served system (FCFS) for the primarily dollar (A/B) quotas would exacerbate the problem. For the auction would provide an attractive alternative for any bananas from Latin America that failed to secure entry under FCFS. There would be a strong incentive to dollar operators to offer highly competitive bids in respect of these surplus quantities rather than to have to ship them on to the much less remunerative markets of Eastern Europe. The ACP would thus lose the security of access hitherto guaranteed under Lomé.

## Caribbean Consultations with the USA

In their determination to find a better solution, representatives from Jamaica and the Windward Islands followed up suggestions from USTR for exploratory bilateral discussions. Their aim was to find a basis for agreement for allocating quotas using a historical reference period. In the end a document was agreed which set out at least the broad parameters of a possible agreement on a historic-based quota. This wedded the US insistence on a pre 1993 reference period for the basically 'dollar' quotas with use of 1995–97 for the quota designed primarily for the ACP. The Prime Minister of Dominica sent this to the Commission as a record of the outcome of discussions with USTR, stressing that it was far from being a Caribbean 'wish-list'. But the paper was both leaked and ostentatiously welcomed in Washington as 'the Caribbean Proposal', although USTR had determined its contents as least as much as the Caribbean. The US press were fed the totally erroneous impression that the Caribbean had 'apparently switched sides' and the *Wall Street Journal* reported 'US officials crowing with glee'.[1] Indeed, the USA was to make much play with this 'Caribbean Proposal' in subsequent negotiations with the European Commission.

It is therefore hardly surprising that it had an icy reception from the Commission and at best highly qualified support from other ACP countries. But a modified version was incorporated in a unified ACP position subsequently submitted to the Commission, which likewise pressed for a historical reference period. Moreover, the Commission took up and incorporated in the final solution one key element of the Caribbean and ACP proposals. This was to allocate licences only to primary importers who purchased their bananas in the country of origin.

## First Come, First Served

By July 2000, fifteen months after the panel ruling, and after more than sixty meetings with interested parties on the issue, the Commission concluded that it was simply not possible to reach agreement on a historical basis for quota allocation. The differences, in particular between the EU and the USA, were too wide to be bridged. But the 1999 panel ruling clearly implied that any historically based system would be vulnerable in the WTO unless it had been agreed with interested parties. The Commission therefore concluded that FCFS offered the best option for settling the dispute, because it dispensed with the need for a reference period. With Council agreement, it then launched an intensive internal study and discussions with interested parties on the feasibility of operating FCFS for a highly perishable commodity like bananas.

The Commission also maintained that if FCFS did not prove feasible, the Community should immediately adopt a tariff-only regime, with no quota restrictions and a single, flat-rate tariff. The Commission therefore invited the Council to give it forthwith a mandate to start negotiations in the WTO to unbind the 75 euros tariff should the conclusion on FCFS be unfavourable. The Council decided instead to wait and see.

Predictably, the Commission found FCFS to be feasible, fair and WTO-compatible. What it proposed was not a simple boat race at the beginning of each fortnightly or weekly quota period. Operators would effectively put in bids for volumes already 'committed' to a vessel. If bids exceeded quota available, the Commission would announce, *while vessels were at sea,* pro rata reductions in the volumes from each shipment that would be admitted.

The Commission now proposed that this system would apply to all three quotas. It dropped its controversial proposal for an auction system for quota C in the light of the strong opposition from the ACP and from the European Parliament. But the C quota of 850,000 tonnes intended primarily, though not exclusively, for the ACP would be subject to a tariff of 300 euros on non-ACP imports. This increase in the preference (from 275 euros) was also in deference to views expressed by the European Parliament.

Although the US government had been prepared to accept some form of FCFS, and had put forward its own suggestions on how this might be applied, it vigorously opposed the Commission proposal, primarily because of the 300 euros duty for quota C. The USA argued that this was equivalent to a separate ACP quota and therefore needed an Article XIII waiver. The Commission denied this and gave a formal undertaking during a WTO meeting that if the tariff proved prohibitive for dollar imports it would be reduced. This failed to mollify the USA, but it inevitably increased the fears of the ACP.

The ACP saw FCFS as a real threat to their survival. It seemed tailor-made for the major trading companies with worldwide sales. These had the flexibility to adjust their shipping and marketing programmes in order to dispose of quantities that were left over once bids had been cut back. The ACP did not, least of all the Caribbean, for whom the Community was the only feasible market. Moreover, the ACP feared that at periods during the year it would pay dollar importers to load maximum volumes on ships at marginal cost and pay the higher tariff on whatever failed to get through on the A and B quotas at 75 euros.

## The Council Legislates

The Commission and the Council were running out of patience. On 19 December 2000, the Council finally adopted legislation that applied a new system of tariff quotas from 1 July 2001 at the latest. It set the volume of the quotas and the tariffs but delegated to the Commission the power to determine the method of quota allocation.[2] It was made clear that this was intended to be by FCFS, although the door was left open for a settlement on the basis of a historic reference period if, contrary to expectations, agreement on this could be reached in time.

The legislation provided for transition to a tariff-only regime not later than 1 January 2006. It also enabled the Commission to reduce the 300 euros tariff for quota C during the transitional period, if it proved discriminatory in its effect.

The Council adopted this legislation in the face of strong lobbying from the ACP countries, appeals from the Caribbean and a statement by the US trade representative, Ambassador Barshefsky, that 'There is no circumstance first come first served could be accepted by the U.S.'

This time round, the UK was not only not in the presidency but also isolated in opposing the legislation. The UK alone voted against it. In a formal statement written into the minutes it warned that 'The latest proposal ... will not end the trade dispute; nor is it evident that the measures to be introduced under it ... will ensure the continued viability of the Caribbean banana export industries. For these reasons, the UK opposes the proposal.'

Other member states broadly supported the Commission proposal for one of two reasons. States that had their own domestic growers were concerned above all to avoid moving directly to a tariff-only system, which they feared might prove the only alternative in the absence of agreement on a quota system. The fear was that this would result in lower market prices and increase the cost of deficiency payments to growers to a level that might prove impossible to sustain within the fixed budget ceiling. Therefore the overriding need was to secure a tariff quota. How the quota was allocated was far less important to them.

Other member states with no domestic production were suffering from 'banana fatigue' and just wanted to see an end to the dispute and to the sanctions as quickly as possible. The one exception, the UK, stood out alone, regardless of sanctions, in defence of the Caribbean and, through them, of the other ACP countries.

## Agreement with the USA

The Commission made one further attempt at a meeting the very next day to bridge the gap with the USA on a historic system, but to no avail. But the New Year brought a glimmer of hope with the installation of a new President and administration in the USA. The new trade representative, Robert Zoellick, was an old sparring partner of Pascal Lamy, who had taken over the previous year as Community Commissioner for External Trade; they also shared an addiction to running marathons. Whatever the reason, the chemistry between them was a good deal better than that between their respective predecessors, Sir Leon Brittan and Ambassador Barshefsky, whose contacts were reputed to have been none too cordial. Be that as it may, in April, just three months into the new US administration, agreement was reached, at last, between the Community and the USA on a historic-based system.

The two-stage move to tariff-only was preserved, with a definitive end to quotas from 1 January 2006, with only a flat-rate tariff, at a rate to be negotiated, to protect the ACP. But changes were agreed in the quotas for the transitional period. The key new proposal was to establish the separate ACP quota that the ACP had always sought but had been told was not negotiable. The USA now undertook to support the necessary waiver in the WTO. But in return for this the ACP had to accept a transfer of 100,000 tonnes from the ACP (quota C) to the dollar suppliers (A/B quotas). Those changes would take effect from 1 January 2002, provided that the WTO waiver had been obtained. Prior to that, quota C would be 850,000 tonnes and be open to imports of bananas from all origins, subject to a tariff of 300 euros on those from non-ACP sources. Allocation in both stages for all quotas would initially be on the basis of imports in the period 1994–96. For quotas A and B, qualifying imports had to be from dollar sources and for quota C from ACP sources.

### Reaction to the Deal

Not everyone was happy with the settlement. Dole had been pressing for an FCFS system. A Dole spokesman said that they 'got sold up the river....the real issue was simply to get a system that would take care of Chiquita'.[3] The settlement was certainly a resounding success for Chiquita, which had been bitterly opposed to FCFS, and should now obtain a market share closer to the level that they had claimed. Ironically, this did not save them from having to file for Chapter 11 protection against bankruptcy proceedings.

Ecuador, which had also supported FCFS, resented not having been consulted before the deal was struck, but subsequently endorsed it. The increase in the dollar quota at the expense of the ACP quota must have been welcome to the world's largest and most efficient dollar banana exporter.

For the ACP there was relief that the quota system had been retained, with allocation on the basis of past performance, rather than FCFS, and they welcomed the separate ACP quota, assuming that the necessary WTO waiver could be secured. But it came at a very high price. Just how high would soon become apparent.

# 17

# Cotonou Complications

## The Cotonou Agreement

Concurrently with the last WTO case and the search for a WTO-compatible solution, the European Community was negotiating with the seventy-three[1] ACP countries for a successor to the Fourth Lomé Convention, which expired at the end of February 2000. This took the form of a 'Partnership Agreement', which was finally agreed in February 2000 and signed in Cotonou, Fiji, three months later.

This Partnership Agreement is radically different from its Lomé predecessors and operates over a much longer period – twenty years. It reflects the Community's desire to replace Lomé with an arrangement that meets the same objectives of combating poverty and promoting sustainable development but in a more WTO-orientated manner. In particular, the Community aimed to replace the non-reciprocal trade preferences of Lomé with a series of economic partnership agreements (EPAs) based on regional free-trade areas. Since the WTO required free-trade area agreements to be reciprocal, this was likely to prove less advantageous to the ACP than the more one-sided, altruistic, Lomé provisions.

The Agreement provides for a preparatory period until 2008, during which the Community would negotiate EPAs with those ACP states able to benefit from them. The Commission would explore other WTO-compatible means of maintaining benefits for those countries not able to do so. Meanwhile, certain current Lomé benefits, including tariff preferences, would continue during the transitional period till 2008.

For bananas, the Lomé commitment was replaced by a new Banana Protocol. This no longer referred to the preservation of traditional benefits of each ACP state in the Community market. The Community's general commitment to maintain the viability of the ACP banana industries was confirmed in Article I, but in somewhat ambiguous terms:

> The Parties recognise the overwhelming economic importance to the ACP banana suppliers of their exports to the Community market. The Community agrees to examine and where necessary take measures aimed at ensuring the continued viability of their banana export industries and the continuing outlet for their bananas on the Community market.

Did this imply an obligation to ensure the continued viability of exports to the Community of even the least competitive ACP country? Did it suffice for measures to be 'aimed' at this objective without actually achieving it? Could these obligations therefore be satisfied by the general provision in the protocol for financial and technical aid designed to enable ACP states to become more competitive? These were soon to become immediate, practical issues, as Chapter 19 will show.

## A Haggle over Waivers

When the Fourth Lomé Convention expired at the end of February 2000 so did the WTO waiver authorising the tariff preferences under Lomé. Although imports covered by Lomé nevertheless continued to enter duty-free, it was essential to legitimise this by a new waiver for the Cotonou Agreement. Both the European Community and the ACP countries therefore submitted a formal request to the WTO for the necessary waiver from the provisions of Article I. The request was made on 29 February 2000, the day before the waiver for Lomé expired.

Perhaps inevitably, this request was seized on as a bargaining counter in the negotiations over the banana regime. It was not finally granted until 14 November 2001, a year and eight months later – and seven months after agreement had been reached on the basis for the new Community banana regime.

Several Latin American countries, including Ecuador, Guatemala, Honduras and Panama, tried to exploit the EU and ACP need for this waiver for Cotonou to squeeze out further concessions on bananas, at the expense of the ACP. Initially, they blocked consideration of the request on technical grounds, arguing that this could not be considered without knowing the final outcome on bananas, even though the request was for a general provision for duty-free entry covering a very wide range of products besides bananas. These countries argued that bananas should be omitted, for the time being, from the list of eligible products. This would have been a high-risk option for the Partnership.

Once substantive consideration at last began in July 2001, these countries tabled proposals for amendment that would again have singled out bananas from other products, by terminating the concession for bananas at the end of 2005, while for other products the waiver would continue until 2008. Again, the argument was that the level of tariff in the subsequent tariff-only regime would not be known till nearer that date. But requiring a new waiver at that critical point would clearly have placed both Community and ACP under duress for the critical negotiations on the tariff level.

Ecuador also sought to disallow duty-free entry for ACP bananas entering under the quotas (A and B) intended primarily for dollar bananas.

The waiver was finally agreed during the WTO Ministerial Conference at Doha, Qatar. It was clear that without the waiver there would be no agreement on launching the new round of multilateral trade talks, which was the primary purpose of that conference. No one wanted to incur the odium of holding up that major development for the sake of such petty manoeuvres. Nevertheless, the waiver was only conceded at a price.

The limitations proposed earlier were dropped, but from 1 January 2006, when the tariff-only regime is due to begin, the waiver would only apply to bananas if the new tariff was at a level 'that would result in at least maintaining total market access' for all WTO member suppliers. An annex to the decision, set out at the end of this chapter, laid down a complex system of arbitration, which could be invoked by any interested party that considered that the new tariff failed to meet this criterion. If the arbitration went against the EU, the waiver would not apply to bananas under the new regime. The agreement provided for both the tariff negotiations and any necessary arbitration to be completed before the new regime was due to begin.

Loss of the waiver could be fatal for ACP banana exports, so this decision presented a formidable hostage to fortune, which could adversely affect the EU and ACP position in the negotiations for the tariff to apply under the new regime.

Ironically, the Article XIII waiver that the Community and the ACP also requested to permit the separate ACP quota under the banana regime was granted without comparable difficulties. The Community had at one time considered this not to be negotiable because there had hitherto only been one precedent for an Article XIII waiver. But it was securing exemption from Article I, governing tariffs, that proved the real problem and has resulted in a potentially serious threat for the future.

---

### WTO Decision of 14 November 2001

The waiver would apply for ACP products under the Cotonou Agreement until 31 December 2007. In the case of bananas, the waiver will also apply until 31 December 2007, subject to the following, which is without prejudice to rights and obligations under Article XXVIII.

- The parties to the Cotonou Agreement will initiate consultations with Members exporting to the EU on a MFN basis (interested parties) early enough to finalize the process of consultations under the procedures hereby established at least three months before the entry into force of the new EC tariff-only regime.
- No later than 10 days after the conclusion of Article XXVIII negotiations, interested parties will be informed of the EC intentions concerning the rebinding of the EC tariff on bananas. In the course of such consultations, the EC will provide information on the methodology used for such rebinding.

In this regard, all EC WTO market-access commitments relating to bananas should be taken into account.

- Within 60 days of such an announcement, any such interested party may request arbitration.
- The arbitrator shall be appointed within 10 days, following the request subject to agreement between the two parties, failing which the arbitrator shall be appointed by the Director-General of the WTO, following consultations with the parties, within 30 days of the arbitration request. The mandate of the arbitrator shall be to determine, within 90 days of his appointment, whether the envisaged rebinding of the EC tariff on bananas would result in at least maintaining total market access for MFN banana suppliers, taking into account the above-mentioned EC commitments.
- If the arbitrator determines that the rebinding would not result in at least maintaining total market access for MFN suppliers, the EC shall rectify the matter. Within 10 days of the notification of the arbitration award to the General Council, the EC will enter into consultations with those interested parties that requested the arbitration. In the absence of a mutually satisfactory solution, the same arbitrator will be asked to determine, within 30 days of the new arbitration request, whether the EC has rectified the matter. The second arbitration award will be notified to the General Council. If the EC has failed to rectify the matter, this waiver shall cease to apply to bananas upon entry into force of the new EC tariff regime. The Article XXVIII negotiations and the arbitration procedures shall be concluded before the entry into force of the new EC tariff-only regime on 1 January 2006.

# 18

## *Winners and Losers*

The WTO passed judgement on the rights and wrongs of the dispute according to its rules on international trade. But this tells us little or nothing about who gained and who lost out as a result of the EU regime. This chapter considers what effect the regime had in the marketplace and on those dependent on it.

### Consumers

Let us start with the end of the chain, the consumer. Before the common regime came into operation the Community was effectively divided into separate national markets, as we saw in Chapter 7. Some countries restricted imports of bananas from Latin America and prices were inevitably higher in those states than in states that placed no restrictions on imports. A tariff quota was bound to raise prices in those states that had not restricted imports and to lower prices in those states that had restricted them, because the latter would have to admit imports from all sources without restraint within the limits of the tariff quota. A common regime therefore implied price convergence.

In Germany, which had strongly opposed the regime, there were bitter complaints over the increase in the price of bananas that it caused. Germany was particularly affected by the introduction of the new regime because it automatically ended Germany's right to duty-free entry for bananas that they had won under a special protocol to the Treaty of Rome. So they had to carry this increase, equivalent to about 20 per cent *ad valorem*, in addition to the impact of the restriction of overall supplies to the Community.

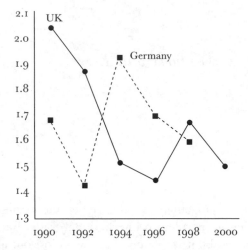

*Source*: FAO, based on the arithmetic average of the twelve monthly averages.

**Figure 18.1**   Retail prices (US$/kg)

The big increase in imports of dollar bananas in 1991 and 1992 had pushed down the average retail price[1] in Germany by nearly 20 per cent (from DM 2.71 per kg in 1990 to DM 2.24). In 1994, the first full year of the regime, the retail price rose by 40 per cent (to DM 3.11), much to the anguish of the press and those most opposed to the regime. Indeed there is evidence to suggest that some traders chose that moment to increase wholesale margins in Germany, thus increasing the initial impact of the regime.[2] But within two years the price had reverted to little more than its 1990 level and subsequently fell well below it (see Figure 18.1).

The UK had the opposite experience, with prices falling from a peak of 118.6 per kilo in 1991 to a low of 91.5p in 1995. Although it recovered from this low point, by the year 2000 the average price had fallen to only 99 pence. Allowing for the effect of inflation, this was equivalent to 73 pence in 1990 – or 38 per cent below the 1991 peak. This trend was to continue, fuelled by the battle between supermarkets (see Chapter 19). By 2003, the UK had the lowest prices in the Community.

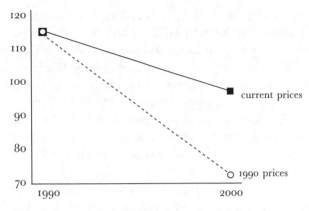

Source: FAO adjusted as retail price index.

**Figure 18.2**   UK retail banana prices (pence/kg)

Overall, the consumer had little cause for complaint about the impact of the regime. It was the producer that bore the strain.

## Companies

Chiquita, then the leading banana trader, had triggered the long battle by invoking US trade legislation to seek redress for the damage it believed that the EU regime had inflicted on it. There is no doubt that Chiquita did lose market share, but how much and why? A study in 1995[3] showed that Chiquita's sales fell from 25 per cent of the Community market in 1991 to 18.5 per cent in 1994. Later FAO figures showed a total fall of about 10 percentage points by 1998. But even this is only half of the loss Chiquita claimed.

In contrast, the two other major US-based companies improved their position under the new regime. The Dole Food Company increased its share in the period to 1994 from 11 per cent to 15 per cent and Del Monte from 7.5 per cent to 8 per cent. By 1998 both had improved further, Del Monte substantially so.

These very different results partly reflected the fact that at the time the regime was introduced Chiquita was already strongly established in the European market, whereas Dole and Del Monte were not. Chiquita saw its established position in Europe threatened and eroded by the operation of the regime, particularly by the seemingly confiscatory nature of the B licences and the adjustments for activity functions. Dole and Del Monte did not have comparable positions under threat and seized the opportunity that the regime presented to take a larger stake in the Community and ACP trade, which the regime was designed to protect. They accordingly acquired an interest in established traditional operators and invested in production in Community and ACP countries.

As a result, the combined stake of the three US-based companies in Community and ACP production rose from 6 per cent in 1992 to 31 per cent in 1994; and the gains of Dole and Del Monte broadly offset losses by Chiquita. US firms on the whole did not, therefore, fare badly, but that was no consolation to Chiquita – and it was Chiquita that, in the end, had the ear of the President and of USTR. In the subsequent tough negotiations over implementing the WTO ruling, US policy was driven by a determination to redress Chiquita's perceived wrongs. The final settlement to the dispute largely achieved this aim. It impressed Wall Street enough to raise the price of Chiquita stock by 50 per cent overnight.[4]

The USA claimed that the EU regime favoured European companies at the expense of American. This was because it provided special measures to help traditional ACP banana exporting countries to maintain their position in the market, and European companies, such as Fyffes and Geest, were major importers of these bananas and were consequently deemed to benefit as a result. But this view ignored the fact that ACP bananas were a great deal less profitable to import than dollar bananas, because they cost up to twice as much at point of origin, cost more to ship to Europe, yet sold in competition with Latin American bananas in the same market.

Fyffes, the largest European importer, did indeed increase its market share threefold between 1992 and 1998, to around 17 per cent of the EU market. But much of that increase was achieved by buying up other companies in Europe, in order to extend its geographical scope, rather than by organic growth. Geest, the other major importer into the UK, presented a very different picture, starkly illustrated by its share price. In March 1993, before the regime began, this was at a peak of 475 pence; it fell thereafter to a low of 107 pence in November 1995. The following month Geest sold off its banana business. The decline in profits that precipitated this sell-off appeared to be primarily a consequence of bad judgements in its operations in Costa Rica and bad luck, in the form of hurricane damage, in the Windward Islands. But the regime did not save it.

In the event, Geest's loss proved a gain for the Windward Islands. Geest Bananas was finally sold to a consortium of Fyffes and Wibdeco, the Windward Island Banana Development and Export Company, which imported all bananas from the islands. Although this entailed Wibdeco incurring a large debt, it gave the company the great benefit of directly controlling marketing and distribution of its bananas in the UK.

## Exporting Countries

### The ACP

An avowed objective of the regime was to fulfil the EU commitment to safeguard the trade of traditional ACP suppliers. Its success or failure must therefore be judged by how far the regime enabled traditional ACP suppliers to maintain a viable export trade.

### The Caribbean

For the Caribbean trade as a whole, the results were bitterly disappointing, particularly in the final years of the regime. In 1990, prior to the introduction of the regime, the seven traditional Caribbean exporting countries (Jamaica, the four Windward Islands, Belize and Surinam) between them provided 360,000 tonnes out of total UK banana imports of 470,000 tonnes. By 2002 they provided only 178,000 tonnes to a much-expanded UK market of about

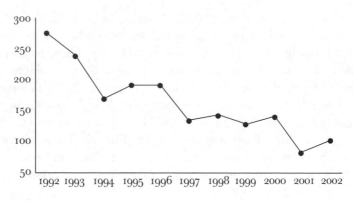

*Source*: National Economic Research Associates, *Banana Exports from the Caribbean since 1992*.

**Figure 18.3**   Windward Islands exports (1,000 tonnes)

750,000 tonnes.[5] Sending lower volumes to an expanding market sharply reduced their market share.

The main cause of this decline was the failure of the regime to yield prices remunerative to the Caribbean. The regime was never given a real chance to operate as intended, because it was constantly being changed, mainly as a result of pressure exerted through the WTO. The Banana Framework Agreement of April 1994 (described in Chapter 11) required a 10 per cent increase in the dollar quota over two years. This depressed prices. Then in 1999 the level of protection for the ACP was substantially reduced as a result of the first WTO ruling and was reduced again by the changes resulting from the final EU–US agreement in 2001.

On top of that, in 2000 the market had to cope with a disastrous influx of additional dollar bananas, over and above the quota, imported illegally through ports in six different member states on forged licences. Although the Commission said that the fraud had been operating since 1996 and the total volume involved was 220,000 tonnes, the main impact occurred in 2000, which was the year that it was discovered. The effect of that extra volume on the market was more severe than anything that had gone before. The Commission put the total duty evaded at

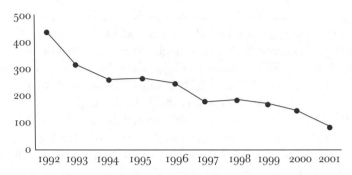

*Source*: National Economic Research Associates, *Banana Exports from the Caribbean since 1992*.

**Figure 18.4**   Windward Islands exports,
real value in local currency (EC$)

160 million euros – about £100 million.[6] However, Community producers were partially compensated for the low prices by the system of deficiency payments (called compensatory aid), which in 2000 accounted for more than half of their income. ACP producers had no such support.

In the Windward Islands, which together constituted the largest of the traditional Caribbean exporters, exports fell from 238,000 tonnes in 1993, the year that the regime was introduced, to 99,000 in 2002, and the number of growers from 24,000 to 7,000 in the same period.[7] By far the biggest exodus of growers occurred in 2001, when almost 4,000 left, 34 per cent of the total. The massive 21 per cent cut in the unit value of their exports in 2000, as a result of the fraudulent imports, was followed by a serious drought which hit production in 2001, and many found this just too discouraging. But the Windward Islands were not the only casualties. In Jamaica one of the three large estates producing for export was closed down, and in Surinam the government-operated banana export company, Surland, shut down following a strike, which was largely the consequence of the low price levels.

In contrast to Jamaica and the Windward Islands, Belize improved its position under the regime. Belize is part of the British

Commonwealth, and was known as British Honduras before it attained independence in 1981. But it is physically part of Central America, bounded by Mexico in the North and by Guatemala in the West and South. Indeed, Guatemala nursed a centuries-old claim on parts of Belize, which it only relinquished in 1991. But the Eastern border of Belize is the Caribbean Sea.

Because of its Commonwealth status, Belize offered a potential supplementary source of duty-free supplies for Fyffes in the 1970s as imports from Jamaica continued to diminish. But the export trade did not really take off until after the industry was privatised in 1986 and a new port was opened up in the south of the country (Big Creek) in 1991 to facilitate banana exports. This major development was financed by private investors, led by Fyffes and the banana growers, and supported by the Commonwealth Development Corporation and Barclays Bank.

Unfortunately, the development of banana production in the south was delayed by climatic problems in 1990 and a subsequent outbreak of Black Sigatoka disease. As a result, Belize fared badly when country allocations were made to traditional ACP suppliers under the new single market regime. It was awarded a country allocation of 40,000 tonnes, which seemed generous in the light of past performance but was far below the country's potential or the level that it deemed necessary to render the investments made economically viable. Good flat land near to the port and substantial mechanised plantations gave Belize the potential to expand, which was held back by this allocation, because it placed a ceiling on the country's exports to the EU as well as ensuring access for them. But the Banana Framework Agreement enabled the Commission to give Belize a modest additional allocation of 15,000 tonnes in 1994 (see Chapter 11).

The end of country allocations for the ACP, following the loss of the first WTO case, should in principle have opened up an opportunity for Belize to increase its exports under the global ACP quota introduced from 1999. But, because Belize did not set up an importing operation of its own in the EU, it did not qualify for export licences in its own right and this imposed a financial if not a physical constraint on expansion. Nevertheless, Belize increased its exports from 25,000 tonnes in 1991 to over 68,000 in 2000. Then a severe hurricane in October 2001 devastated the plantations, but exports recovered in 2003 to exceed previous levels.

## West Africa

Francophone West Africa prospered under the regime. While Caribbean exports declined, those from the Ivory Coast and Cameroon more than doubled between 1990 and 2000. Why did these countries fare so much better? Partly because they were better endowed by nature in the topography of the land and the quality of the soil. They did not suffer from the structural and geographical problems that affected the Windward Islands. But because production was stimulated by investment by the dominant trading corporations, particularly after the single market provided an additional incentive for this. By the end of 1997, Dole controlled 60 per cent of export production in both countries through major shareholdings in local companies. Del Monte and Chiquita also developed smaller stakes. These companies were well placed to take advantage of the Community's aid programmes for restructuring and improvement – there was plenty of flat land available for expanding. As a result of these investments, production and marketing in these two countries was much improved, their production costs were much lower than in the Caribbean, and their larger volumes brought economies of scale. They were therefore much better placed to cope with the lower prices

In addition, in spite of the single market, France, which is the main market for West Africa, seemed better able to maintain price levels than the UK, on which the Caribbean relies. This may partly reflect the greater competition between supermarkets in the UK (see Chapter 19) but also, perhaps, a greater devotion by the populace to products of francophone origin. This consumer preference certainly appears to be a potent factor in Spain, where retail prices have also remained much higher than in the UK or Germany, reflecting the consumer loyalty to bananas from the Canary Islands.

## Dominican Republic

The Dominican Republic has also been a major beneficiary of the regime. The Dominican Republic started with token exports to the EU of only 4,000 tonnes in 1990 but reached 60,000 in 2000, overtaking Jamaica for the first time. As the Dominican Republic was not a traditional ACP supplier, it initially had no traditional quota volume, but they were granted a special allocation as a result of the BFA. Subsequently, the WTO ruling that ended country allocations to traditional ACP suppliers enabled the Dominican Republic to increase exports under the single quota provision for all ACP countries. Moreover, the Dominican Republic took the lead in exports of organic bananas, both to the Community and to other countries. By 2000 its organic banana exports of 44,000 tonnes made it by far the world's main supplier of organic bananas.[8]

**Latin America**

Changes had been taking place in Latin America in the years before the start of the EU regime. Production greatly increased from the late 1980s onwards, leading to a surplus of bananas. Moreover, as explained in Chapter 8, the major companies expected the prospective common market regime to impose a quota on imports, and each therefore sought to establish the highest possible base for the calculation of its future share. This led to changes in market share between Latin American countries. In particular, Ecuador, the largest and lowest-cost producer, nearly doubled its exports to the Community between 1990 and 1992, increasing its share of total EU imports from 13 to 22 per cent.

Once the regime was in operation, the tariff quota placed an effective ceiling on total imports from Latin America. This started at 2 million tonnes, which was the average of dollar imports in 1989–91, although appreciably below the 1992 peak. But it was later increased by stages to 2,553,000 tonnes as a result of the Banana Framework Agreement (BFA), described in Chapter 11, and also to provide for the three new member states that joined in 1995.

The BFA effectively required half of the entire dollar quota (49.4 per cent) to come from the four signatory countries – Colombia, Costa Rica, Nicaragua and Venezuela. This is likely to have distorted trading patters within Latin America. Certainly

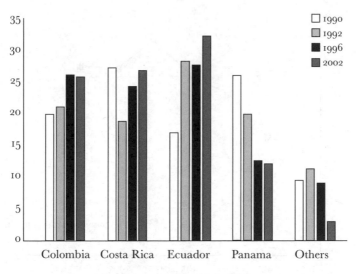

*Source*: Eurostat and national statistics.

**Figure 18.5** EU imports (% of $ total)

its two significant members, Colombia and Costa Rica, did well, each attaining a peak of over 26 per cent of the dollar imports. Panama, which was not a member, fared less well. It is Chiquita that exports most of Panama's production and it may well have been the potential impact of the BFA that finally provoked Chiquita to seek legal redress in the USA.

Figure 18.5 compares the market share of each of the main players in the crucial years before the regime (1990 and 1992), after the BFA was in operation (1996) and in 2002.

The effect of the regime on Ecuador is more difficult to assess. Ecuador's total banana exports worldwide rose by consistent annual increases from under 2.2 million tonnes in 1990 to a peak of almost 4.5 million tonnes in 1997, after which climatic and other problems affected export production (see Figure 18.6). Whether Ecuador would have sold much more to the EU if the BFA did not exist is not certain. Although Ecuador is the largest single

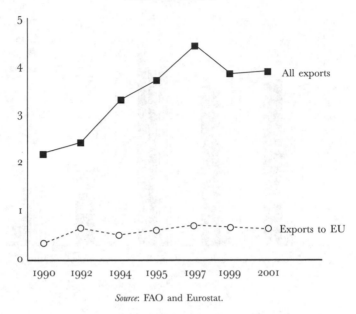

*Source*: FAO and Eurostat.

**Figure 18.6** Ecuador exports (1,000 tonnes)

supplier to the EU, the EU is not its principal market, as Figure 18.6 shows. While the EU offers higher prices, the West Coast of the USA has the attraction of a much shorter shipping distance and avoiding the cost of passage through the Panama Canal. Nevertheless, Ecuador has fought tenaciously for unrestricted access to the EU banana market.

The dollar quota was fully used and there is little doubt that had there been no tariff quota Latin American exports to the EU would have been greater and prices lower. How far that would have benefited growers is uncertain. In the increasingly cut-throat competition for market share the prize tends to go to those whose workers accept the lowest pay.

# A Threatened Future

## The Price of Peace

The EU–US deal contained two major threats to the ACP. The more distant, but potentially the most lethal, was the final termination of the quota regime at the end of 2005. This was foreshadowed from the very beginning of the negotiations. It was seen as a precondition for any transitional quota. But this was a purely political decision, based on a judgement of what was negotiable in the light of the WTO rulings, not on the needs of the ACP. It was totally at variance with the view of the European Parliament, which had earlier called for a transition period of ten years, more than double that actually conceded; and which had insisted that there should be no automatic transition to a tariff-only regime. Parliament wanted this final step to be decided only after, and in the light of, a review of the impact of the transitional arrangements on EU and ACP producers and adoption of any supplementary measures that the review showed to be necessary. But while the European Parliament now has power in several key policy areas, such as the budget, to oblige the Council of Ministers to take account of their views and to hammer out a compromise, there is no such obligation in respect of the banana regime. The Council had to receive the opinion of Parliament but not necessarily to follow it.

The commitment to end the tariff quota regime put in jeopardy the future of the Caribbean banana industry. ACP bananas would continue to enter the EU free of duty, so the tariff to be applied once quotas were removed would provide their one

protection against cheaper imports from Latin America. But the
level of the tariff remained to be negotiated, nearer the time, in
accordance with the provisions of the GATT and there was no
guarantee that this would be high enough to enable the ACP
trade, and that of the Caribbean in particular, to survive in the
absence of any limit on the volumes entering the market. Given
the structural surplus of bananas in the world, higher volumes and
still lower prices seemed inevitable. So total uncertainty remained
beyond the brief period of transition. It could mean the end of
the industry in the more vulnerable ACP countries.

The more immediate threat to the ACP trade arose from
changes to the tariff quotas. In return for the waiver permitting a separate, exclusive, quota for the ACP, the existing ACP
provision of 850,000 tonnes was cut by 100,000 tonnes. That
volume was simply transferred to the dollar quota. Superficially,
this appeared both reasonable and painless, since the ACP had
never used the whole of their quota; total EU imports from the
ACP rarely exceeded 750,000 tonnes. But since the whole of the
augmented dollar quota *would* be used, this transfer resulted in
an increase in the total volume on the market. Predictably, this
seriously depressed prices.

The effect was to render permanent much of the oversupply
caused by the illegal imports described in the preceding chapter.
The impact of those imports was reflected in a sharp fall in the
unit value of exports. For the Windward Islands the average fell
from US$530 per tonne in 1999 to US$420 in 2000, a fall of 21
per cent. The EU–US agreement effectively consolidated much
of the oversupply that had caused this collapse and thus removed
any prospect of a significant recovery in price.

In June 2002 the ACP Council of Ministers addressed a formal
resolution to the EU Commission and Council warning that the
new regime had 'resulted in prices plummeting to levels which
threaten to displace ACP suppliers, most of whom have no alternative markets'; and that this was 'already creating tremendous social
and economic dislocation and eroding the achievements in the fight
against poverty'.[1] In practice, this problem could only be resolved
by some reduction in the quota, but the Commission insisted that
a reduction was simply not politically feasible.

## The Supermarket Squeeze

This oversupply affected prices throughout most of the Community, but in the UK market, on which the Caribbean depends, the problem was made much more acute by the continuing battle for market share between supermarkets. Some saw ever-lower prices for bananas as the means of attracting more customers into stores, and the additional volume of bananas on the market served to sharpen this competition. For eager sellers in a buyers' market enabled supermarkets to increase the pressure on their regular suppliers. They could now dictate prices to traders rather than negotiate them. Since supermarkets account for about 80 per cent of UK banana sales, the impact has been severe.

The situation deteriorated sharply after the US company Wal-Mart took over the UK supermarket chain Asda. Asda decided to obtain its entire banana supply from a single trader and to select that supplier on the basis of a competitive tender. This role could only be filled by a company sourcing bananas from large-scale plantations in Latin America. Del Monte won the contract, after a hotly contested battle, at a highly discounted price. In 2003 the contract was renewed for a further two years at a price reported to be even lower.[2] The Asda initiative led to a damaging series of competitive price reductions from August 2002.

The previous chapter showed how retail prices for bananas in the UK had already fallen substantially over the previous ten years – from an annual average of 114.1 pence per kilo in 1990 to just 99 pence in 2000, equivalent in real terms to a fall of 64 per cent over the decade. Moreover, while prices had been falling costs had been rising, not only with inflation but also because supermarkets made increasing demands on suppliers for new and more complex forms of packaging and presentation, such as mixing different degrees of ripeness in a single pack.

As a result of the price war that began in August 2002, the average price in supermarkets had fallen again by the spring of 2003 to 88 pence and in June and July several chains – Asda, Tesco, Sainsbury and Morrisons – were competing at 79 pence.[3] This accelerating price squeeze affected banana producers everywhere. Even in 2002, the unit value of banana exports from the Windward Islands in local currency was already 40 per cent lower than in 1991,[4] but the situation now deteriorated further.

The logic behind this downward spiral was spelled out by Sainsbury's banana buyer, Marcus Hoggarth, in an interview with a trade journal in July 2003: 'With all our staple lines, the aim is to re-assure the customer that they are getting the best deal in the market place.' He argued that customers don't necessarily shop at only one supermarket chain and that they would notice 'consciously or otherwise' any discrepancy between chains in the prices of core lines.[5] In fact, a study in 1996 had shown that over half of consumers either were 'not sure' of the price they paid for bananas (20 per cent) or 'had no idea at all' (35 per cent).[6] Possibly consumers had become more price-conscious since then, but the lower prices had little effect on consumption. By the summer of 1993 the price at multiples for loose bananas, which account for 70 per cent of the market, were down 27.5 per cent on their price a year earlier, but sales were up by only 1.56 per cent.[7] This 'destructive price-matching conga'[8] thus produced only a minuscule increase in sales but had a devastating impact on growers in the producing countries. However, its primary objective had been to win – or at least to hold on to – customers rather than to increase sales. As Marcus Hoggart put it: 'Although we have good strong relationships with our suppliers, when push comes to shove the balance tips to the consumer.'

At the time of writing this collapse of prices had already led to casualties in the industry. Surinam's government-owned industry ceased exporting in 2002 following a strike indirectly caused by the squeeze on prices paid to producing countries for green bananas. Attempts were being made to revive the trade but the low price levels could well discourage the necessary investment. Jamaica also cut back export production, closing down one of its three large estates producing for export, because prices were no longer remunerative. The whole Caribbean industry struggled to survive at the lower price levels that flowed from the settlement. The future was very uncertain.

## A Race to the Bottom?

The parlous situation on the EU market since 2002 was largely the consequence of adverse WTO rulings and the need to find alternative means of helping the ACP that were acceptable to the victors in the WTO disputes. The EU struggled long and tenaciously to secure the best deal that they could for both their own producers and the ACP. In the nature of things, they were better able to secure the first objective than the second. The final deal was a striking demonstration of the constraints imposed by the WTO on the way that help may be given to developing countries.

Moreover, the outcome of the dispute will not necessarily benefit all the producing countries in Latin America who challenged the regime. The fierce competition between supermarkets, and the consequent scramble between banana trading companies for their custom, increases the downward pressure on prices. For a commodity in surplus, where labour is a large cost element, this in turn increases the threat to the level of wages and working conditions in the supplying countries that win, as well as to employment and living standards in those countries whose growers are forced out of business. Untrammelled free trade is not always an unmitigated blessing.

This problem is seen at its most acute in Ecuador. According to a recent study, banana workers' wages there were around $5 per day, but many only got work for two or three days a week and workers rarely received the benefits in kind, like housing and health care, that are common on plantations in other countries.[9] Strikes aimed at improving pay and conditions have been crushed by physical violence from hooded gangs armed with guns.[10] In Nicaragua pay is even lower, by a substantial margin, but Ecuador accounts for about a third of world banana exports and this therefore puts pressure on others. The president of Chiquita's International Division, no less, had complained of the competition and that in Ecuador 'there are no unions, no labour standards and pay is as low as two dollars a day'.[11] Ultimately, it is the cut-throat competition between supermarkets, fuelled by a world surplus of bananas, that stimulates this aptly dubbed 'Race to the Bottom'.

## EU Obligations

The plight of the Caribbean following the EU–US deal cannot be reconciled with the commitment in the Fourth Lomé Convention, that under any common regime adopted for bananas no traditional ACP exporting state 'would be placed as regards access to, and advantages in, the Community, in a less favourable position than in the past or at present'. But that Convention expired in February 2000.

Since that commitment was made in December 1989, a number of factors had affected the attitude of the EU on this issue. One was the enormous volume of work and disproportionate amount of time, energy and tension devoted to the banana dispute with such unsatisfactory results. This led to increasing 'banana fatigue' among both Commission and member states and a passionate wish that the problem would just disappear. They fervently hoped that the agreement reached after the seemingly endless negotiations with the USA had finally put an end to the saga.

A second factor was the diminishing influence in the EU of the sense of obligation to former colonial territories fostered by France, the UK and Italy. The more countries with no equivalent concern acceded, the less sympathy this could command. The scheduled expansion to twenty-five member states in May 2004 would decisively tilt the balance against them.

Third, and most important, was the change in the Treaty relationship between EU and the ACP. The Lomé Convention was superseded by the Cotonou Partnership Agreement (see Chapter 18), which stressed the need for EU support for the ACP to be compatible with WTO rules. It provided for the negotiation by 2008 of economic partnership agreements (EPAs), of which a key feature would be reciprocal, two-way (though not necessarily equal) concessions. For ACP countries unable to meet these requirements, other possibilities would be explored, but partnership and reciprocity would be the model, anything else an exception and almost certainly inferior.

For bananas Cotonou was far less specific than Lomé. Under the Banana Protocol, quoted in the preceding chapter, the Community only 'agrees to examine and where necessary take measures aimed at ensuring the continued viability' of the ACP banana export industries and to ensure a continuing outlet for ACP bananas on the EU market. *This still implied responsibility to ensure the survival of the ACP banana export trade, including that of the Caribbean.* For Cotonou, like Lomé, was an agreement between the EU and each signatory ACP state. But the European Commission maintained that it was fully meeting its commitments by providing a more attractive market than elsewhere through the operation of the regime. It argued that those who were not efficient enough to cope should take advantage of the aid being offered to improve their act or to divert into some other economic activity.

Lawyers may argue whether the Commission position was consistent with the Cotonou agreement, in the letter if not in the spirit. From the Community viewpoint it made sense in a shrinking and increasingly competitive world. But it raises a disturbing question. The Windward Islands, which are the most vulnerable of the ACP banana exporting countries, have very little current or potential alternative source of income apart from tourism. The problem is particularly acute in Dominica, which is the most dependent of all on bananas and has the least alternative resources. Moreover, the banana industry is important to the economy of the Windward Islands not only for its substantial direct contribution to export earnings, but also because it alone renders economic the weekly shipping service on which other exports depend and which is also vital for imports. Diversification is therefore only feasible alongside a core banana export trade.

A Royal Commission drew attention in 1939 to the striking contrast between the beauty of the island and the great poverty of the population (see Chapter 6). That poverty was largely eliminated by the successful development of the banana export trade to the UK under the benevolent protection of a regulated market. But if the banana trade cannot survive in the harsher conditions imposed by the WTO rulings and the way that the EU has applied them, that poverty could return. Yet the trade involved is minuscule in world terms. The Windward Islands now export under 100,000 tonnes a year. This is only 0.9 per cent of world trade in bananas and 2.5 per cent of the EU market. Can it really be necessary to do so much damage to these small vulnerable economies rather than make special arrangements to cater for them? Is this really a necessary price to pay for free trade?

## What the EU Could Do

The European Commission has undertaken to submit a report to the Council on the operation of the banana regime by the end of 2004. This report will include an assessment of 'the extent to which the most vulnerable ACP suppliers have been able to maintain their position on the Community market' and, 'if appropriate', proposals to adjust the operation of the regime.[12] However, since the regime will then have barely a year left to run, such changes would probably be of limited value. Moreover, the Commission indicated that, during the second half of 2004, negotiations would begin under Article XXVIII of the GATT for the single tariff to apply from 2006. The Commission reiterated that transition to tariff-only on 1 January 2006 was a decision already made.

If the tariff quota regime is indeed to be brought to an end, it will be crucial that the single tariff that is to replace it as the sole protection for the ACP should be fixed at a level high enough to enable all the ACP banana-exporting countries to maintain their place in the market. But that will depend on the outcome of negotiations with interested parties under the GATT (Article XXVIII).

Failing agreement on an adequate tariff, it would seem morally incumbent on the EU to find other means of fulfilling its commitment under the Cotonou Agreement to ensure the continued viability of the ACP banana industry. But WTO rulings and the EU–US agreement of April 2001 leave very few options. One solution would be to retain an effective tariff quota beyond 2005 in spite of the EU–US agreement to end it. That would require a more flexible attitude by the USA and Ecuador as well as the enlarged EU. But there have been signs that the depressed market conditions since the EU–US agreement have made not only all the ACP countries but even some of the larger trading corporations reluctant to see the EU market subjected to the risk of a free-for-all. The state to which the market has been reduced might just conceivably make the unthinkable more negotiable. But the WTO rulings would render this impossible without the agreement of all major parties.

The EU commitments are to each ACP country and the EU should therefore take account of the disparities between them. Just as Latin American producers are more competitive than ACP growers, so Cameroon, the Ivory Coast and the Dominican Republic are much lower cost producers than the Windward Islands or Jamaica. A tariff that enabled West African producers to remain in the market could nevertheless spell disaster for the Caribbean. It would not be right to adopt a solution that catered only for the strongest. Differentiation to cater for exceptional cases is a nettle that might have to be be grasped.

In the case of the Caribbean, there is only one way that the EU can live up to the letter and spirit of their commitments. That is to abandon past hang-ups and reservations and accept the need for some form of direct aid to the most vulnerable growers, whether in the form of subsidised inputs or deficiency payments. This is what the USA urged after the first WTO case, when they suggested 'negative tariffs'. The Commission proposed similar direct support, albeit as a temporary measure, to safeguard small ACP growers against possible adverse consequences of transition to a single market.[13] It is the one sure means to preserve a specific and limited market volume for small growers who are so highly dependent on it. Such help could be linked to realistic requirements on the beneficiaries to reduce costs.

Unfortunately, there are no grounds for optimism. With ten Eastern bloc and other candidate countries newly admitted in 2004, these issues will be decided by a very different European Union. The new member states bring with them no historical ties with the Caribbean or with the ACP generally and a desire to secure at the lowest possible price imports of foodstuffs that they do not themselves produce.

# 20

# *Prospects for Survival*

## Narrowing the Gap

Nature and geography make it impossible for Caribbean banana producers ever to compete on equal terms with Latin America, for the reasons explained in Chapter 3. But there has been an explicit assumption that, in return for the protection provided by the EU, ACP suppliers would strive to improve their ability to compete. The House of Commons Select Committee that reviewed the negotiations for the first EU regime spelled this out clearly in their Report of February 1993:

> It is not in our view realistic to expect the ACP to compete on equal terms with the dollar producers by 2000 or maybe ever; but *it is important from everybody's point of view that the maximum efforts should be made, and seen to be made, to narrow the gap.* (stress in original)

Political leaders in the Caribbean shared this view. In October 1992 Prime Minister John Compton of St Lucia argued that the proposed Community regime 'will buy us vital time during which we will be able to continue to improve our banana growing and marketing and compete more effectively with the Latin American producers'.

The previous UK national regime provided little incentive for improvement because the market was too well protected. The important exception was quality, in which the monitoring committee imposed by the Ministry of Agriculture brought about substantial improvements. But the single market regime did create pressure to increase efficiency, particularly following the loss of the first WTO case and subsequent appeal in 1997. This obliged the Community to end cross-subsidisation through the B licence system and to abandon individual country quotas for the ACP. The former led to lower prices for ACP producers; the latter removed the guaranteed access for specific volumes allocated to each traditional ACP supplier and thus exposed the higher-cost Caribbean producers to greater competition from lower-cost ACP countries, notably the Ivory Coast, Cameroon and the Dominican Republic.

The need to achieve improvements became more urgent following the failure of the second WTO case in April 1999. For it soon became clear that the most that could be salvaged was a modest transitional regime before the end of all protection other than a tariff preference. That left very little time to take the necessary measures. But what had been done, meanwhile, to take advantage of the schemes on offer in order to prepare, so far as possible, for the more difficult times ahead?

## West Africa

In Cameroon and the Ivory Coast a great deal had been done. This owes much, as Chapter 18 explained, to investment by the dominant trading corporations, particularly after the single market provided them with an additional incentive, through the B licence system, to import bananas into the EU from ACP countries. In addition, these US-based multinationals were able to draw on Community funds for aid for substantial investments in cableways, drainage, irrigation and other improvements under the Special Framework of Assistance, which was designed to make ACP banana production more competitive. There is no doubt that these improvements have helped to reduce the competitive gap between West African and Latin American production.

## Dominican Republic

The Dominican Republic has successfully carved out for itself a niche market in organic bananas, having rapidly become the world's leading exporter of this speciality (see Chapter 21).

## The Caribbean

**Belize**

Belize cannot match the scale of production in West Africa and, like other Caribbean suppliers, has a longer shipping distance to its markets. It is also subject to the hazards of wind chill, which periodically affects production. Nevertheless, Belize alone among the traditional Caribbean suppliers succeeded in increasing its exports to the EU under the regime. Its export production comes from a small number of plantations of viable size, which have the potential for survival after 2005, provided the tariff provides sufficient additional protection to compensate for the loss of the tariff quotas. Indeed, with a high enough tariff, Belize might arguably be better off without the quotas, because this would remove its current problem of having no entitlement to import licences in its own right.

Import licences are granted only to operators established in the EU. Belize was not in a position to follow the example of the Windward Islands and Jamaica, which had their own companies (Wibdeco and Jamaica Producers) in the UK. It sold its bananas under annual contracts with Fyffes, who took over ownership of them on board ship in Belize (f.o.b.). It was therefore Fyffes that earned the licence entitlement. This suited Belize very well initially because volumes were too small to justify setting up its own operation in the UK. Surinam had a similar arrangement, for the same reasons. But a number of factors combined to change this. The expansion of production in Belize, the introduction of a single global quota for the ACP, which in principle provided scope for them to increase their exports, and the harsher commercial climate that developed all served to render Belize dissatisfied with this dependence on licences owned by others.

To meet these concerns, the Caribbean Banana Exporters Association, in agreement with the importing companies, approached the European Commission jointly with the Belize government in December 2000 to press for changes to the Community legislation that would enable Belize to qualify to receive licences solely on the strength of having produced bananas for export to the Community. But the Commission declined to adopt this suggestion, probably because of concern over the consequences of applying these changes to other ACP countries.

In a tariff-only regime there would be no place for licences. In principle, there would also be no bar on Belize achieving its long-cherished goal of exporting 100,000 tonnes a year, the level originally deemed necessary for economic viability at the time of the major investment in the port at Big Creek. Since then there has been substantial investment, with help from Community funds, in improving plantations through drainage and irrigation and planting improved varieties of banana. In addition the area under bananas has been increased and the government has built an all-weather road (the Southern Highway) linking the plantations with the port at Big Creek. But the industry will still require a substantial tariff preference to have a realistic chance of flourishing or even surviving in a tariff-only regime.

## Jamaica

Jamaica has sought to adapt to the more difficult market conditions by concentrating its production for export on its two remaining large estates. These now account for about 90 per cent of Jamaican banana exports. Smaller growers in Jamaica operate under conditions similar to those in the Windward Islands. They have turned essentially to the domestic market, which has less exacting standards and now takes two-thirds of total Jamaican production of around 135,000 tonnes. Bananas are sold locally both as a staple vegetable, while they are still green, and as a fruit when ripe. Community aid has been devoted to raising standards of growers through technology transfer and replanting; to encouraging increased cultivation of plantains through better disease control; and to developing alternative uses for the banana and its by-products, such as banana chips and packaging materials.

The best fruit from the smaller growers goes for export alongside the product of the two major plantations, and makes an important contribution to their returns. But the export trade has difficulty surviving under the low prices prevalent under the revised regime. The future will depend entirely on there being a tariff or other measures capable of generating a more sustainable price level.

## The Windward Islands

In the Windward Islands production has always been far too fragmented, yields far too low, and productivity seriously impeded by lack of adequate irrigation facilities. The results were variable volumes and quality with high production and shipping costs.

There is also a curious cultural handicap that has its origins in the subsistence farming from which much of the industry developed. This is the strongly embedded tradition that on farms the working day ends around noon, when the heat reaches its zenith. This means that growers that need to hire labour pay a full day's wage for four to five hours' work and cannot cater for activity later in the day. Why this tradition should apply in the banana fields but not elsewhere, such as on sugar plantations, is a mystery. But it has cost implications that are more difficult to sympathise with than those arising from physical factors such as topography and size.

There has been a massive exodus of growers from the industry in the Windward Islands. Numbers declined from about 24,000 in 1992 to around 7,000 ten years later, as growers became discouraged by low prices and by constant threats to the survival of the Community regime. (These are summarised in the Appendix.) The biggest fall came in 2001, when the double blow of record low prices in 2000 followed by losses from drought led 4,000 to give up. This exodus was not the result of a planned scheme of rationalisation, based on early retirement and diversification, for which Community aid was on offer. It reflected spontaneous and individual grower reaction to falling returns and diminishing prospects. Those who left were not necessarily the least able growers. We do not know what happened to them thereafter. Many would have been part-timers with other sources of earnings. For others the options would have been to turn to other crops or subsistence farming, to seek alternative employment, possibly in the tourist trade, to join the growing number of unemployed, to emigrate, or to indulge in illicit pursuits like drug trafficking.

We know that cultivation of ganja, as marijuana is called there, has become an increasing problem in the Caribbean and particularly on the island of St Vincent, where it has become the mainstay for a significant part of the population.¹ There is also evidence that, faced with the many hazards of an illicit trade, some ganja farmers hanker wistfully after the days when they could rely on bananas as the number one crop.² But for them ganja does what bananas failed to do: it provides them with a living.

The exodus of growers, together with hurricane damage, cut export volumes to less than half the pre-regime levels. This inevitably resulted in loss of some established market share, which is probably irretrievable given the high cost of Caribbean bananas. The only hope for the future lies in concentrating production on a much smaller number of more efficient producers, able to raise their yields to a minimum acceptable level and to accept the increased disciplines dictated by the marketplace.

There has been no shortage of aid funds available, in principle, to help finance necessary restructuring and diversification. In 1994, in the context of the adoption of the common market regime, the Community provided for programmes of aid for restructuring and improvements to the banana industries in ACP countries. This was followed in 1998 by a further ten-year programme in the light of 'the special efforts required as a consequence of the new market conditions', meaning the revised regime which came into effect on 1 January 1999 as a result of the WTO ruling.

Yet there is a yawning gulf between the good intentions of the EU legislators and what happens in practice on the ground. Formidable bureaucratic hurdles have to be cleared to secure agreement to aid applications, with proposals often requiring both local vetting by the Commission office in the region and reference by them back to Brussels. Even when projects are approved there are long delays in disbursing funds: payments under the 1999 scheme were still outstanding in 2003.

More critical was the failure of the Windward Islands themselves to make the best use of the programmes that were agreed. Wibdeco, the Windward Islands Banana Development and Export Company, is responsible for marketing production from the islands. Wibdeco is owned partly by the four island governments and partly by the growers' associations of each island. The professional management had for years sought to bring about the radical changes required to enable the industry to survive in the increasingly difficult circumstances emerging form successive WTO rulings. But it was constantly frustrated by opposition from individual growers' associations and by governments unwilling to back locally unpopular decisions, however necessary they might be for the survival of the industry in the medium term.

The difficulty of dissociating bananas from local politics has been a perennial problem in the islands. Bananas are politically important not only because of their contribution to the economy but also because production tends to concentrate in 'banana belts', where the banana vote can determine the outcome of an election. As a result, attempts by Wibdeco to bring greater commercial discipline to the industry were frequently undermined by the short-term concern of politicians to shelter growers from the chill winds of commercial reality. This simply postponed the day of reckoning.

A Production Recovery Programme, agreed in 1998, was designed in principle to restore the Windwards' production to a level of 200,000 tonnes, through investment in drainage and irrigation combined with restructuring of the industry. Some effective irrigation schemes were carried out, notably in St Vincent, which led to increases in yields on the farms concerned. But topography and lack of water in the dry season limit the potential for irrigation to only a small proportion of the land growing bananas.

Elsewhere much of the funds was frittered away on less essential but more popular purposes such as purchases of trucks and other projects not necessarily related to banana production. These and other failures fostered disillusion and distrust among the vital Community development staff, stationed in Barbados, who were responsible for approving aid programmes in the Eastern Caribbean. There was talk of 'throwing good money after bad'.

Following the settlement finally reached between the Community and the USA, Wibdeco presented to the industry in May 2001 a new set of proposals 'For the Development of a Modern, Sustainable Windward Islands Banana Industry'. The plan entailed concentrating export production on farms that had been certified as conforming to specified husbandry standards and that were capable, after installation of irrigation, of attaining a yield of at least 30 tonnes to the hectare. This would be a great improvement on the current average yield of under 20 tonnes but would still be far short of the level in Latin America of around 50 tonnes. Certified growers or local growers' associations would be required under contract to supply at least a specified minimum volume per shipment and regular weekly supplies. Managerial structures and staffing throughout the industry would be streamlined, and staff numbers reduced by two-thirds as a result. All technical and financial aid to the industry would be concentrated on these targeted growers. The aim was to supply exports of 115,000 tonnes a year from these farms.

Three years later, only very modest progress had been made and key elements remain to be implemented, including commitment to firm volume contracts and elimination of unproductive units. But the only hope for the survival of a viable industry in the Windward Islands lies in radical rationalisation, such as that proposed. The crucial need is to concentrate the export industry on a much smaller core of the best producers with plots of sufficient size and yield to guarantee regular supplies. Unfortunately it is not always the best growers who occupy the best lands, but it may not be politically or commercially feasible to do much about that. However, funds are available under the Community aid programme for the proposed investment in infrastructure and to assist those farmers who will have to leave the industry. Whether the necessary political will exists to bring about such a radical change remains to be seen.

# 21

# Equitable Trading?

## The Market

The future of the Caribbean banana trade depends on three elements. First is the regime that will finally emerge for 2006, including the degree of tariff protection that this will provide. That depends primarily on the EU. Second is the improvements that the Caribbean countries themselves must achieve in increasing their competitive ability through rationalisation and improved productivity. Third, but no less important, are the market opportunities. These will largely be determined by the supermarkets.

Given the structural surplus in the world, prices on an unrestricted market will not be remunerative for the Caribbean. If the tariff preference is their sole protection, this may well not be high enough to bridge the gap that will always remain, for geographical reasons, between their costs and those of Latin American producers, with their large plantations, better terrain and economies of scale – or indeed between the Caribbean and other ACP countries. Caribbean survival would therefore depend on *whether the market can be induced to accept that price should not always be the sole or overriding criterion for purchase.* Only the supermarkets can determine this, since they account for over 80 per cent of sales in the UK, which is the only established market for Caribbean bananas.

## Equitable Trading

### Fair Trade

This principle has already been accepted in the form of Fair Trade products. The concept of 'Fair Trade' goes back thirty or forty years. The aim is to enable and encourage consumers to buy products with the assurance that these have been produced in a socially and environmentally friendly way. This means that growers and workers received a reasonable return for their labour; and that workers on plantations enjoyed specified minimum social benefits and amenities and the right to membership of a democratically elected trade union.

Equally, the Fair Trade movement seeks to ensure that crops are cultivated in a manner that respects the environment, notably by limiting use of pesticides and fertilisers and avoiding pollution of watercourses or damage to natural habitats.

Many consumers are willing to pay a premium price for Fair Trade products because of the moral satisfaction they derive from the assurances that the Fair Trade label provides. Similarly, consumers are willing to pay a premium for organic bananas as for some other organic foods, because they believe that they are better for their health or more friendly to the environment – or both.

The Fair Trade (FT) standards are laid down by a central body, Fair Trade Labelling Organisation International, and national or regional organisations in Europe and North America award the FT label and monitor performance of producers that meet them. The premium on Fair Trade Products is intended for investment in social and environmental improvements. The FT label cannot, however, be granted to the whole of the output of growers who achieve FT standards, because there is a limit to the proportion of FT bananas that the market will take at this social premium.

Fair Trade bananas first appeared in the Netherlands in 1996 and within a few months had captured 10 per cent of the Dutch banana market. They subsequently spread into Switzerland and several Community countries, including the UK. Initially supplies came from Ghana, Ecuador, Colombia, Costa Rica and the Dominican Republic, but in August 2000 the Windward Islands also started exporting Fair Trade label bananas to the UK, supplementing existing FT imports from Latin America. In that year, the UK became the second largest market for Fair Trade bananas, following Switzerland. By 2003, the Windward Islands were supplying over half (54 per cent) of the FT bananas sold in the UK, with the Dominican Republic the next largest supplier at 21 per

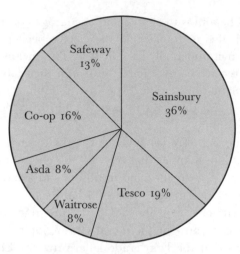

Source: Trade information.

**Figure 21.1**    Supermarket Fair Trade banana sales
in the UK, 2003

cent. Among leading supermarkets, Sainsbury had the lion's share
of FT banana sales in the UK in 2003, as Figure 21.1 shows.

In the UK, Fair Trade bananas have risen from only 1 per cent
of banana sales in 2000 to nearly 3 per cent in 2003. Experience
in the Netherlands and Germany suggests that following an initial
enthusiasm, sales tend to declin~.[1] But UK forecasts for future
growth have varied from 5 per cent of the market by 2006[2] to a
possible ultimate ceiling of 10 per cent or more.[3] Even so, given
the competition, that would still provide an outlet for only a part
of the Caribbean output. However, much depends on the sales
policy of the major supermarkets and how far they wish to promote Fair Trade produce.

**Organics**

The Dominican Republic took the lead in developing organic
bananas and in 2001 provided over half the global supply. Other
Latin American countries also export them. In 2002, one UK
supermarket chain encouraged Grenada, the smallest of the four

Windward Islands, to dedicate land to a range of organic fruit and vegetables, including bananas.

Yet conversion to organic production takes three years. During this period organic methods are used, normally entailing higher costs and lower yields, but products do not earn a price premium. Moreover, there is no guarantee that premiums will be as high once conversion is complete as they were at the outset. Initially production was almost exclusively from small growers but there are now large-scale plantations in the Dominican Republic and Ecuador.[4] If this trend continues, it is likely to bring down premiums.

In 2000 the UK became the largest market in Europe for organic bananas, importing 17,000 tonnes out of the modest European total of 42,500 tonnes. (Germany was second with 11,000 tonnes.) Organic bananas accounted for about 5 per cent of the UK market, compared to just over 1 per cent in the Community as a whole.

Indeed, the UK has shown rapid growth in sales of organic food generally. Fruit and vegetables and groceries together accounted for about 65 per cent of these in 2000/01, but dairy products (27 per cent), meat (3 per cent) frozen foods (2 per cent) and even beer and wines (2 per cent) were included.[5] This growth may well reflect the impact on consumer psychology of the successive health scares concerning salmonella in eggs, listeria in cheese, and above all BSE in cattle, none of which was underplayed by the media. But the rate of increase has been declining.

Organics, like Fair Trade, could only, at best, sustain a proportion of total Caribbean banana production. The major part of that production will still need a viable market, if income and employment are to be maintained. Moreover, only that main body of production can provide the volume necessary to render a weekly shipping service economically viable. Without that volume, there would be no economic means of shipping the niche products. *That is why the niche markets would provide an important supplementary outlet, but can be no substitute for the main banana trade.*

### A Caribbean identity

Most Caribbean banana production is very close to the ideals and requirements of Fair Trade bananas, even though the limited volumes that can be marketed as FT would prevent them from receiving the FT label.

In the Windward Islands, in particular, production is mainly on very small family farms, often on hilly terrain, where production is necessarily labour-intensive and relies less on chemical inputs than under more industrialised systems of production. Much of the labour is self-employed and that which is not receives fair wages in accordance with local labour laws. Production is therefore both environmentally and socially friendly. Moreover, the high degree of dependence on this one crop confers a special social importance on supporting the industry. These are features of Caribbean production that make it important to establish a separate identity for Caribbean bananas with the aim of securing recognition in the market of this ethical dimension.

To some extent, this process has already begun and some supermarket chains are establishing direct links with specific designated growers in the Windward Islands who undertake to conform to their production guidelines. This is an encouraging development, but how far it will prove possible to build a sufficient market for Caribbean bananas at an ethical price depends on the extent of the support – both from the all-powerful supermarkets and from consumers.

## The Crucial EU Factor

Over all this hangs the dilemma that neither better farm structure and rationalisation nor the best possible marketing strategies will save the Caribbean industry unless the EU fulfils its obligation to provide terms of access that will enable all traditional ACP exporting countries to continue trading.

# Reflections on the WTO

The banana war shone a revealing light on the way in which the WTO operates. The procedures for settling disputes were laid down in the Disputes Settlement Understanding (DSU), which has been described as 'the single greatest achievement of the Uruguay Round',[1] because it established, for the first time, effective machinery to ensure application of international trade law. But the experience of the ACP states in the banana dispute both revealed unsatisfactory features of some DSU procedures and pointed to the need to review some of the GATT rules themselves.

The Caribbean states were shocked by the outcome of the WTO cases. Prime Minister Edison James of Dominica forcefully articulated this feeling in a speech following publication of the results of the appeal of September 1997:

> We feel betrayed by the WTO, because we joined the Organisation believing that its primary purpose was to bring about improved living standards and equity and fairness in international trade; that it would be one which would ensure that the rule of the jungle in which the powerful ride roughshod over the smaller members of the trading community would not be condoned. What we find is that the WTO has ended up by being a system in which the legitimate interests of small countries will always be sacrificed once they conflict with those of the major players.[2]

The GATT includes a number of provisions permitting preferential treatment of developing countries, such as the Generalised System of Preferences (GSP) and preferential treatment in various ways for the least developed countries. But for the purposes of the banana dispute the only relevant special provision that could help the ACP countries was the general facility under Article XXV for a waiver from specific rules. In the event this played a key part in the resolution of that dispute. But the experience demonstrated that it is the dominant trading blocs, particularly the USA, that call the tune. The crucial waiver from the provisions of Article XIII became a realistic possibility only once the USA, which had originally opposed it, agreed to support it as part of the final deal.

Moreover, that waiver came at a very high price for the ACP, both in the specific terms imposed for the transitional period and, above all, in the EU commitment to a free market, subject only to an unspecified flat tariff, after the brief period of four years.

The inarticulate anti-globalisation protests that began at Seattle were partly fuelled by the impression that the few dominant powers were using the WTO to penalise the slightest deviation from free-trade rules when it suited their interest to do so, regardless of the consequences for small states. The much-publicised dispute on bananas reinforced a growing unease about the role being played by the WTO and other international bodies.

The Caribbean perception that the outcome of the proceedings was unjust was heightened by the way in which the WTO procedures appeared to be manipulated against the Caribbean states at the behest of the USA.

## Procedures

The procedural problems in the WTO cases on bananas were disturbing because of the attitude they revealed. Chapter 13 explained how Caribbean and other ACP states were refused full rights of participation, on the grounds that the dispute was between the EU and the USA and other complainants. It is difficult to understand this ruling, in a case that so vitally affected their economies and even threatened their political and social stability. But because complainants, including the USA, opposed this request, these states were relegated to the same status as any other third country with no direct involvement in the trade in question.

This blow was compounded by the eviction of the Windward Islands' private legal advisers from the proceedings of the first WTO panel at the request of the complainants on the grounds that they were not permanent government officials. Significantly, the decision to limit representatives to permanent officials had been taken at a meeting from which the ACP had been excluded. But why should an island with only 70,000 inhabitants be *required* to employ trade lawyers as permanent officials and how could they be expected to afford it? The appeal body by its own example showed its disagreement with the panel's action, and the right of states to appoint whomever they wished as delegates was subsequently confirmed. At least this was one small success derived from the banana dispute, though at a price.

The experience in this case suggests either undue rigidity in the rules themselves or a lack of imagination and flexibility on the part of the chairman or of his advisers, from the permanent WTO Secretariat, who strongly influenced proceedings. Unfortunately, both panel members and Secretariat staff tend to come from the same small pool of countries. The three-man panel comprised the Hong Kong permanent representative to the GATT, a senior official from the Swiss Federal Office for Foreign Affairs and an Australian economist known for his free-trade views. In cases where small and vulnerable developing countries have a major stake in the outcome, it would be better to have on the panel at least one person who has personal experience and understanding of the problems they face.

Proposals have been tabled in the Doha Round of negotiations to improve third party access to dispute proceedings. It is to be hoped that small, vulnerable states in particular will be given every reasonable opportunity and help to safeguard their interests in such cases.

## Sanctions

The most dramatic and publicised outcome of the 1999 proceedings in the banana dispute was the WTO authorisation of US sanctions against the EU for non-compliance. It seems absurd that the WTO authorises members to impose crippling penalties on businesses

totally unrelated to the trade at issue, resulting in serious hardship
for individual companies, particularly small family firms, both in
the countries offending and in the country imposing retribution.

Indeed the WTO panel also authorised Ecuador to impose sanctions exceeding $200 million in value; and Ecuador arguably had
a stronger moral case to do so, since it had at least followed the
proper procedure of first challenging the revised EU regime in the
WTO. But Ecuador did not apply sanctions, apparently because to
do so would have inflicted severe damage on its own economy. A
similar situation subsequently arose over the EU dispute with the
USA over corporate tax breaks given to US companies in respect
of gains from exports. The WTO awarded the EU the right to
sanctions on up to a staggering $4 billion of trade annually. The
effect on both sides of imposing sanctions of that size would be
enormous and unpredictable and the EU wisely opted to hold its
hand, at least initially. There must be a more sensible and civilised
way of dealing with such issues.

It has been suggested that industries penalised should at least
be in the same sector as the product in contention. But a more
attractive idea was put to a House of Lords committee by two
distinguished economists, who suggested that compensation should
take the form of obligatory liberalisation by the offending state
rather than additional trade restrictions by the winning party.[3] This
seems both a more equitable approach and one more consistent
with the spirit and objectives of the WTO, which is to foster and
liberalise trade.

Unfortunately, this has little prospect of adoption in the fore-
seeable future because it is a fundamental right of each state to
decide how to implement WTO rulings. The WTO can authorise
a wronged state to impose sanctions but cannot itself impose a
solution on the offending state or even fine it for non-compliance.
To do so would conflict with the principle of the sovereign independence of each contracting party. Within the EU, both the
Commission and the Court of Justice exercise such supranational
powers. But such a pooling or transfer of sovereignty to a wider
international arena, even in a severely circumscribed form, would
be a quantum leap for which the international community may
not yet be ready.

It was interesting to note, however, that trade sanctions did not prevent the banana ruling from taking over two years to implement. This long delay was due not to foot-dragging but to the inherent difficulty of reconciling major differences between the many interested parties.

## Vulnerable States

Although the dispute was essentially between the USA and the European Union, those with most at stake on both sides of the argument were all developing countries. In the case of the Caribbean, these included developing countries that were also small and economically vulnerable. This is not a question of comparative wealth per capita. One developing country might be less poor than another, but nevertheless be more economically vulnerable because its economic viability rests on a single product, such as bananas in the case of the Windward Islands. Similarly, the small size of population (in the region of 100,000 in each state), remoteness from markets, lack of natural resources and proneness to climatic disasters are all factors that contribute to economic vulnerability.

From the Treaty of Rome onwards, the EU has increasingly recognised, in principle, the need for special differential treatment of peripheral regions of the Community to take account of handicaps imposed by 'their remoteness, insularity, small size, difficult topography and climate, economic dependence on a few products, the permanence and combination of which severely restrain their development' (Article 299 [previously 227] of the Treaty of Rome as amended at Amsterdam in November 1997). The same factors argue in favour of special treatment in the field of international trade for states with similar handicaps.

Largely as a result of the banana dispute, there is now some recognition of the case for greater flexibility in the WTO's treatment of small and highly vulnerable states. The House of Commons International Development Committee recommended in 1988 that the UK government 'urge the WTO to consider the inclusion of a 'vulnerability/small state' category in its rules which might qualify for special and discriminatory treatment'.[4] Subsequently, there was broad acceptance in the Doha Round of trade negotiations 'that special and differential treatment for developing countries shall be an integral part of all elements of the negotiations'.[5] But there is much less agreement on special dispensations, in particular for states with small vulnerable economies (SVEs), and still less on what form these might take.

The very first step of defining an SVE is a major stumbling block. According to a recent study, the World Bank and the Commonwealth Secretariat have wrestled for years with this 'conceptually difficult and politically fraught' problem.[6] This has been a subject of continuing negotiation in the context of the Doha Round. According to the WTO Secretariat, size of population has been the most popular indicator so far proposed, but ideas of qualifying size range from 1.5 million to 5 million. Other factors considered relevant include shares of global trade, size of gross domestic product (GDP), transport costs, and lack of scope for economies of scale.[7] It is hardly surprising that everyone remotely eligible wishes to be in on the act, so that reaching an agreed definition will not be easy. No one wishes others to gain advantages that might adversely affect their own trade. The danger is that failure to reach agreement on a definition might make it impossible to give the necessary help to those that are most self-evidently small and vulnerable.

For example, the four Windward Islands have a population averaging around 100,000 per state, compared to 1.5 million, which is the lowest parameter currently being considered. These island states are highly dependent on one product, bananas, and are distant from their only feasible market. Their scope for diversification is also extremely limited as they have few natural resources. Their case for special, differential treatment seems indisputable.

There is also much debate about the nature of the special differential treatment that small vulnerable states should be granted. A number of proposals have been made, some of which would certainly have helped in the banana dispute – and could still do so. For example, on WTO procedures, proposals include improving access of such countries to WTO dispute proceedings in which they are third parties and, more radically, providing funding to enable such states to establish and maintain missions to the WTO in Geneva.

There are also proposals to exempt these states from the requirement that benefits in regional free trade agreements should be reciprocal and safeguard their existing preferences in required moves towards greater liberalisation. Such concessions could be helpful for the more vulnerable ACP states in the move towards regional agreements or other arrangements scheduled under Cotonou.

The banana dispute has placed a crucial industry in the Windward Islands under threat as the result of WTO rulings. If this major source of income is lost, some other form of employment and earnings must be found. Service industries of various kinds and information technology have been suggested. But to build up almost any alternative industry requires a degree of protection, just as the dominant developed powers, and the USA in particular, built up industries behind protective barriers before embarking on the crusade for free trade. There is some recognition of this in a proposal to enable SVEs to maintain subsidies to offset their cost disadvantages, but much more will be needed to give SVEs a fair chance of surviving the rigours of the further liberalisation currently envisaged.

There is equally a need to enable developed countries to grant differential benefits to SVEs without having to obtain a special waiver. For example, if some form of tariff quota could be retained in the EU, it would be a significant benefit for the Windward Islands, which are the most vulnerable suppliers, to have a country allocation to ensure them a place in the market, notwithstanding the inhibiting rules on allocation elaborated by the WTO panel during the dispute. Similarly, under a tariff-only regime, it should be permissible for the EU to provide a 'negative tariff' or subsidy to small vulnerable states to enable their trade to survive under a single tariff that would otherwise provide inadequate protection. Exemption from the rules in such cases, as of right, would help SVEs without causing harm to others, provided only a very small share of trade was affected.

In the harsh world of international trade politics it is difficult to be optimistic about the prospect of securing the necessary support for such initiatives. Nevertheless, since Doha is specifically a 'Development Round' it would be sad indeed if no progress was made towards making the rules more sensitive to the needs of small vulnerable economies.

## Fairer Trade

The most difficult question raised by the banana dispute is whether anything can be done at international level to mitigate the risk of a 'race to the bottom' for producers of a commodity in world surplus in a free market, a race stimulated by the increasingly fierce competition between supermarkets (see Chapter 19). There is a marked contrast between WTO insistence on absolute parity of treatment between contracting parties in the terms and conditions of imports and its almost total indifference to the conditions under which those imported goods are produced. The Fair Trade movement is making some headway in getting consumers to accept the relevance of social and environmental conditions of production in determining the fair price of a product. But this is entirely on a voluntary basis and inevitably affects only a small proportion of trade, because there is a limit to the volumes that can be sold at the Fair Trade premium.

The interesting question is whether the WTO will ever reach the stage of permitting differential – and therefore discriminatory – terms of access reflecting such factors as observance of International Labour Organisation (ILO) standards for treatment of workers or of production methods designed to protect the environment. There are non-governmental organisations pressing for provisions of this kind, but securing their embodiment in international trade rules is likely to prove a long haul.

# 23

## *Post-mortem*

The banana dispute absorbed considerable resources on all sides
in litigation and propaganda and temporarily embittered relations
between the USA and both the EU and the Caribbean. It was
a dispute that nobody wanted and few could have foreseen. It
ended with the Caribbean banana trade close to collapse. Was
it worth it?

The adoption of this controversial banana regime should be
judged in its contemporary context rather than with the benefit
of hindsight. It was broadly comparable to other EU regimes
designed to help the ACP that were already in operation, such
as those for rum, beef and, above all, sugar – none of which
had run into similar problems. Indeed the Caribbean and other
ACP countries had hoped to secure arrangements much closer to
the sugar model, precisely because these offered a much higher
degree of protection, including an undertaking to purchase specified volumes from each ACP country concerned at guaranteed
prices. However, sugar had the advantage of historic arrangements
endorsed by an International Sugar Agreement and accepted by
the USA, which had long operated its own highly restrictive import
regime to protect its domestic sugar producers.

The banana regime did include one novel and highly controversial element in the B quota arrangement, which allocated 30
per cent of the dollar quota to importers of EU or ACP bananas.
But even this was broadly based on precedents of 'twinning', under
which imports of ACP products were encouraged by the reward
of licenses to import the same product from more competitive
origins free of import levy. Indeed the Commission's original ideas

put forward in May 1992 had been on those more traditional lines, but were widely and rightly regarded as too complex and difficult to apply.

Such protective measures had traditionally been justified on the grounds that they gave necessary help to developing countries. There had been intermittent bilateral complaints by Ecuador against the UK national regime on bananas and occasional trade reprisals, but nothing more. Twenty years before the 1992 negotiations for the banana regime, the USA had complained in the GATT about the continued UK restrictions on imports of bananas and other products from dollar areas long after the shortage of hard currency that originally justified them had ended. But the UK defended these quotas on the grounds of Caribbean need. A GATT panel was appointed which invited the two countries to settle this complaint bilaterally and specifically charged them in doing so 'to find a settlement that would pay due regard to the Caribbean countries concerned'. An amicable settlement was reached and the dollar quotas continued, although they were increased. Interestingly, the panel's final report in July 1973 noted that 'although the settlement reached did not fully satisfy the Caribbean countries, the governments of the two parties gave an assurance that they would continue to safeguard, to the fullest extent possible, the interests of these countries'. This concern on the part of the panel contrasts with the tone of the subsequent WTO disputes.

The 1993 regime was being devised at the time of the Uruguay Round of trade negotiations that led to the creation of the new WTO, with its much tougher Dispute Settlement Procedure and its stronger ethos of trade liberalisation. It will be recalled from Chapter 9 that the form of the regime took account of progress in the Uruguay Round discussions by opting for tariff quotas. But it is doubtful whether anyone anticipated the rigour and radicalism with which the new body would interpret the rules.

Moreover, there was no reason to expect the USA to put its considerable weight behind an attack on the regime. The USA had indicated during the negotiations for the regime a strong preference for tariffication, which was the approach that the EU finally adopted. Moreover, although US firms traded in Latin American

bananas, the USA itself did not export them. This made it all
the more surprising that the USA should make a major issue of
the banana regime and spearhead the attack on it. That is why
there was so much speculation in the USA itself on whether its
position on this owed something to the political influence of Carl
Lindner and the generosity that he and his associates had shown
to the political parties.

In spite of internal controversy, the Community went to great
lengths to fulfil its Lomé commitment in the single market. The
regime adopted in 1992/93 met ACP needs, including those of
the Caribbean (apart from a technical glitch that led to oversupply in the second half of 1993), as well as of EU growers. But
things began to fall apart following the first cases in the GATT
in 1993/94 and the fatal EU gambit of the Banana Framework
Agreement to buy off the opposition. This achieved the double
feat of weakening the regime while infuriating Chiquita and others
adversely affected by it. Then came the shock of the loss of the
WTO case and appeal in 1997. Thereafter, the effectiveness of
the regime was progressively undermined by successive salvage
operations, in 1998/99 and 2001, intended to protect it against
the risk of further challenge in the WTO. What finally remained
offered only a pale shadow of the support provided to the ACP
by the 1993 model.

Nevertheless, the regime did provide a framework within which
the West African industry was able to expand and the Caribbean
industry at least to survive, albeit on a much smaller scale and
with increasing difficulty in the final years. From the point of view
of the ACP as a whole, clearly the regime was therefore worth
the hassle. Without it the ACP might have been exposed to unfettered competition from Latin America, with no protection but
the bound tariff. However, the question remains whether similar
or better results might have been achieved less painfully. This
is impossible to answer since one cannot predict what the reaction of the complainants might have been to a slightly different
regime that was less provocative and less disruptive to individual
trading companies.

It might have been possible, for example, to get away with the
tariff quotas and separate allocations for each ACP country if there

had not been the controversial B licences and the bureaucratic complexity of the adjustment of allocations according to activity functions. But it is more likely that the Latin Americans, though not necessarily the USA, would have challenged any restriction that the EU imposed unilaterally on their access to the single market unless it was patently WTO-compatible.

The interesting speculation is what would have happened had the EU sought from the outset to agree a regime with the other parties, who did indeed ask for discussions at the time. It seems very likely that a better deal could have been achieved for the ACP at that stage than was subsequently imposed on them as a result of the EU–US Agreement of April 2001. For the USA was not then fully engaged in the dispute and there was none of the rancour later created by the WTO battles. Above all, the EU did not then have ranged against it the weight of the subsequent WTO rulings, which were more radical and stringent than many informed observers would have expected. On the other hand, whatever might have been acceptable to Latin America and the USA at that stage would almost certainly have fallen far short of ACP demands and expectations, even though it was far better than the current position. But in 1992, no Caribbean banana-exporting state could ever have imagined that the WTO, which did not even exist at that time, would be able to render nugatory the assurances given in the Fourth Lomé Convention and endorsed by eighty-three countries; or how diminished would be their place in the EU market a decade later.

# Afterword
## by Edison James

When this book is published the banana wars will have entered their final and decisive stage. The European Commission is expected to announce imminently its proposals for transition to a tariff-only regime. These will cover both the timing of the transition, which could take place well ahead of the committed date of 1 January 2006, and, most crucially, the level of the proposed tariff. It is around the latter that battle is likely to be waged in earnest.

The EU's undertaking to move to a tariff-only system never implied abandoning the Community's commitment to its traditional ACP suppliers. On the contrary, that commitment had only recently been reaffirmed in the Cotonou Agreement. The intention was simply to switch to a form of support that was more acceptable to current international trading principles. The tariff should therefore be pitched at a level that will maintain current prices and not force traditional suppliers out of the market. Unfortunately, not all the major players seem prepared to accept this approach.

The debate on the tariff will doubtless fuel the popular campaign against any perceived barrier to free trade. But support for a more liberal trading system must be tempered by an understanding of the potential adverse effects that precipate action will have in specific cases. In the Windward Islands, as a result of the battles in the WTO, banana exports have fallen by more than half. But the trade is still vital, socially and economically. For small countries like my own, with a tiny population and barely any natural resources, there is little alternative employment or source of earnings. For those forced out of the banana industry, the choice is therefore between poverty and migration, leading to increasing depopulation.

The country had hitherto been able to earn its way and safeguard the well-being of its people through its long-standing banana trade with the UK; then the heavy hand of the newly created WTO rendered this all but impossible. This book has pointed to the lip service paid in international fora to the need for special consideration for small, vulnerable economies, such as the Windward Islands. The moment has now arrived for the international trading community to put these sentiments into practice, to provide a fair deal for such economies. In the current test case of bananas, it must show the flexibility necessary to ensure by an adequate tariff or other means that the vital Caribbean export trade can be maintained under the new regime.

*The Hon. Edison James,*
*former Prime Minister of Dominica and spokesman*
*on bananas for the Caribbean Economic Community*

# A Climate of Uncertainty

An important, intangible, element affecting the success or failure of the EU banana regime has been the palpable climate of uncertainty that has reigned from the outset, reinforced by constantly declining support. This has served to discourage necessary investment throughout the Caribbean and prompt many growers, particularly in the Windward Islands, to leave the industry.

This appendix lists the remorseless series of threats and challenges aimed at the regime from before it even came into operation and which is likely to continue at least into 2005. This did not provide an encouraging climate for radical, costly and painful measures of improvement and rationalisation.

**June 1992 to May 1993**   Challenge in the GATT by five Latin American countries, which resulted in the panel ruling condemning those national regimes that restricted imports from Latin America. Although the national regimes were about to be superseded, the ruling boded ill for the new regime starting on 1 July 1993, which included key features condemned by the panel (Chapter 10).

**May 1993 to July 1994**   Germany sought an injunction from European Court of Justice to block the introduction of new single market regime. The injunction was refused, but uncertainty prevailed until the substantive case was heard and the German claim dismissed in the summer of 1994 (Chapter 9).

**July 1993 to January 1994**   GATT challenge by the same five countries immediately after the inception of the regime. The panel condemned key aspects of the regime, including the tariff preference for the ACP and the B quota system. Although adoption of the panel report was blocked, its ruling posed a continuing threat (Chapter 10).

**October to December 1993**  Collapse of market prices in UK because of oversupply. This led to concerns that the regime would not provide a viable return to the Caribbean industry.

**April 1994**  The Banana Framework Agreement (BFA) agreed at Marrakesh provided for changes to the regime that significantly reduced protection for the ACP. These included a lower tariff on third-country imports and higher quotas for dollar bananas (Chapter 11).

**September 1994 to April 1995**  Chiquita's Section 301 Petition led the US trade representative to press for drastic changes to the regime, which would have undermined the support on which ACP imports depended (Chapter 12).

**Summer of 1994**  Major campaign by Germany and others, ultimately unsuccessful, to use the impending enlargement of the EU as a reason to reduce the proportion of bananas allocated to cross-subsidise ACP bananas under the B quota system.

**1 January 1995**  Sweden, Finland and Austria acceded to the European Community. The tariff quota was increased by 350,000 tonnes to cater for their needs. Combined with the increases conceded under the BFA, this proved too much for the market and depressed prices. None of the acceding countries had any historic link with ACP countries or had banana growers of their own. This tilted the balance of opinion in the Community against protection. Even before accession, the Swedish Minister of Agriculture had announced her ambition to get rid of the banana regime.

**April 1996**  The USA and Latin American countries launched WTO proceedings against the regime (Chapter 13).

**April 1996 to September 1997**   The WTO panel proceedings and subsequent Appeal ruled against fundamental elements of protection for the ACP. Because the new WTO rules made the panel ruling binding, this was a particularly fraught period for the ACP (Chapter 13).

**September 1997 to June 1998**   The EU explored possibilities for a WTO-compatible new regime to apply from 1 January 1999. Initially Germany, Sweden and other member states backed a US call for a much more liberal regime, with no quantitative restrictions and just a low common tariff. This would have been fatal for the ACP and was not acceptable to the Commission.

**June 1998**   The EU adopted a revised regime, with greatly weakened support for ACP and particularly the Caribbean (Chapter 14).

**November 1998**   The USA threatened trade sanctions against member states because of the regime (Chapter 14).

**January 1999**   As the new regime began, the USA announced the imposition of sanctions from 3 March and Ecuador challenged the regime in the WTO (Chapter 14).

**April 1999**   The WTO ruled against key aspects of the revised regime and authorised US sanctions (though at a much lower level than those the USA had already imposed unilaterally). (Chapter 14)

**Summer 2000**   The Commission found that about 222,000 tonnes of bananas had been imported illegally, using forged licences.[1] This additional volume had a devastating effect on prices, reflected in the deficiency payments paid to Community producers, which provided 60 per cent of their total return. ACP growers received no deficiency payment and had to rely on the market price (Chapter 18).

**April 1999 to April 2001**   Negotiations to try to find a basis for a new regime acceptable to main interested parties. The EU threatened to introduce first-come, first-served as the basis for licence allocation, in the absence of agreement on an alternative, or else immediate adoption of a tariff-only system. Either would have been disastrous for the Caribbean (Chapter 16).

**April 2001 to February 2002**    The EU and the USA agreed in April 2001 on a transitional regime. Negotiations continued till February 2002 on details vital to the ACP. First came the struggle to secure waivers in the WTO to permit both the tariff preference and the separate ACP quota (Chapter 18). This was not finally resolved till November 2001. Then, a strong lobby, led by Germany, sought to transfer a significant share of licences from ACP operators to 'non-traditional operators' who by definition had no previous track record in importing from ACP countries. A compromise highly unsatisfactory to the ACP, and particularly the Caribbean, was finally imposed in February 2002.

**February 2002 on: unresolved threats**    From 2002 the over-supplied market consequent on the 2001 agreement posed a threat to all ACP suppliers. But far from reducing the quota, the Commission was committed to increase it further to cater for the accession in May 2004 of ten new member states from Eastern Europe and the Mediterranean. There was good reason to fear that the additional quota would in practice undermine the market in existing member states, to which much of the additional supplies were likely to be diverted.

Towards the end of 2003, the Commission raised the possibility of moving directly to tariff-only at the time of enlargement on 1 May 2004. This would have brought sudden death to the Caribbean industry, unless the tariff was fixed at a level that provided adequate protection.

Whatever the date of transition to tariff-only, the need for adequate protection through the tariff or other measures remained a critical issue for the Caribbean.

# Notes

PRO documents are in the Public Record Office, Kew.

## Chapter 2

1. Information in this chapter on the origins of the UK trade is derived largely from: A.H. Stockley: *Consciousness of Effort*, limited edition printed privately by W.H. Smith & Son, 1937; Patrick Beaver, *Yes! We Have Some: The Story of Fyffes*, Publications for Companies, Stevenage, 1976; Peter N Davies: *Fyffes and the Banana: A Centenary History 1888–1988*, Athlone, London 1990; S. May and G. Plaza, *The United Fruit Company in Latin America*, National Planning Association (USA), 1958.
2. The Jamaica Fruit Importing and Trading Company, established 1896.
3. The author has followed the formula used by Roy Jenkins, a former Chancellor of the Exchequer, in his admirable biography of Winston Churchill, to provide broad modern monetary equivalents. He multiplied by fifty for the early 1900s, by thirty for the late 1920s and the 1930s and by twenty-three in the immediate post-Second World War period. Roy Jenkins, *Churchill*, Macmillan, London, 2001.
4. Stockley, *Consciousness of Effort*, p. 33.
5. Ibid., p. 57
6. Ibid., p. 69.

## Chapter 3

1. *Report of the Imperial Economic Committee on the Marketing and Preparing for Market of Foodstuffs produced in the Overseas Part of the Empire, 3rd Report: Fruit*, 1926, Introduction, p. 9.
2. Ibid.
3. Interview with the *Jamaican Gleaner*, quoted in A.H. Stockley, *Consciousness of Effort*, W.H. Smith & Son, 1937, p. 137.
4. C.V. Black, ed., *Jamaica's Banana Industry*, Jamaica Banana Producers' Association, Kingston, Jamaica, 1984, p. 75.

5. Ibid., p. 77.
6. West India Royal Commission 1938–39, *Report*, June 1945, Cmnd 6607, ch. II, p. 18.
7. Black, *Jamaica's Banana Industry*, p. 84.
8. Ibid.
9. Harry Browne, *Joseph Chamberlain, Radical and Imperialist*, Longman, London, 1974, p. 79.
10. PRO CO 852/333/4, Letter to Ministry of Food.
11. Peter Hennessy, *Never Again: Britain 1945–1951*, Jonathan Cape, London, 1992, p. 274.
12. Ibid.
13. D.W. Rodriquez: *Bananas: An Outline of the Economic History of Production and Trade with Special Reference to Jamaica*, Government Printer, Kingston, Jamaica, 1955, p. 30.
14. West India Royal Commission, *Report*, ch. XVII, p. 303.

## Chapter 4

1. Peter Clegg: *The Development of the Windward Islands Banana Export Trade*, Society for Caribbean Studies Annual Conference Papers, vol. 1, 2000.
2. PRO CO 852/902/3.
3. Denning Report; see Chapter 6.
4. Lawrence Grossman, *The Political Ecology of Bananas: Contract Farming, Peasants and Agrarian Change in the Eastern Caribbean*, University of North Carolina Press, Chapel Hill, 1998, p. 68; also author's interview with former Chairman of Wibdeco, the Windward Islands Banana Development and Export Company.
5. Memorandum submitted by the Windward Islands Banana Growers' Association to the House of Commons Agriculture Committee, 1992. Printed in their First Report, Session 1992/3, *Arrangements for the Importation of Bananas into the United Kingdom: Interim Report*, HMSO, London, December 1992, p. 37.
6. West India Royal Commission 1938–39, *Report*, June 1945, Cmnd 6607.

## Chapter 5

1. PRO CO 554/990.
2. PRO MAF/393/8.
3. PRO FCO 67/351.
4. PRO FCO 67/349.
5. Patrick Beaver, *Yes! We Have Some: The Story of Fyffes*, Publications for Companies, Stevenage, 1976, p. 90.
6. Iris Freeman, *Lord Denning: A Life*, Hutchinson, London, 1993, p. 337.

7. Denning Report, PRO BT 241/2089.
8. Ibid.
9. Merged in 2001 into a new Department for Environment, Food and Rural Affairs (DEFRA).
10. Anthony J. Payne, *Politics in Jamaica*, Hurst, London, 1988, p. 75.

## Chapter 6

1. The Import of Goods (Control) Order of 1954.
2. *The Queen* v. *The Secretary of State for Trade ex parte Chris International Foods Limited*, Judgment transcript.
3. Memorandum submitted by the Banana Export Company of Jamaica to the House of Commons Agriculture Committee, 1992–93 Session, First Report, *Arrangements for the Importation of Bananas into the United Kingdom*, HMSO London 1992.
4. Quoted in Prof. McInerney and the Lord Peston, *Fair Trade in Bananas?*, Agricultural Economics Unit, University of Exeter, December 1992, p. 32.
5. Henry. S. Gill and Anthony P. Gonzales, 'Economic Consequences of a Banana Collapse in the Caribbean', paper prepared for the Caribbean Banana Exporters Association 1995, ch. 5.
6. House of Commons Agriculture Committee, *Arrangements for the Importation of Bananas into the United Kingdom*, p. 131, para. 217.

## Chapter 7

1. Single European Act, 1986, Article 13.
2. PRO BT 241/2098, December 1973.
3. Lomé IV Convention, Article I.

## Chapter 8

1. Dr David Hallam and Professor the Lord Peston,*The Political Economy of Europe's Banana Trade*, Department of Agricultural and Food Economics, University of Reading, January 1997, p. 25.
2. Ibid., p. 44.
3. Prof. McInerney and the Lord Peston, *Fair Trade in Bananas?*, Agricultural Economics Unit, University of Exeter, December 1992, p. 15.
4. Thomas P McCann, *An American Company: The Tragedy of United Fruit*, Crown, New York, 1976, p. 59.
5. Ibid., p. 208.
6. *Wall Street Journal*, vol. 215, no. 111, quoted in Fyffe's Response to the Section 301 Petition, exhibit J (see Chapter 12).

7. S. May and G. Plaza, *The United Fruit Company in Latin America*, National Planning Association (USA), 1958, ch. 4.
8. McInerney and Peston, *Fair Trade in Bananas?*, p. 9.
9. *Washington Post*, 2 June 2002, quoting US/LEAP.
10. Provided by Banana Link.
11. R.H. Stover and N.W. Simmonds, *Bananas*, 3rd edn, Longman, London, 1987, p. 426.
12. McCann, *An American Company*, p. 75.
13. Quoted in Hallam and Peston, *The Political Economy of Europe's Banana Trade*, p. 22.
14. Stover and Simmonds, *Bananas*, p. 426.
15. Hallam and Peston, *The Political Economy of Europe's Banana Trade*, p. 35.

## Chapter 9

1. Institute of Commonwealth Studies Folder 97 5/4/2, CBEA Minute of meeting with the UK Permanent Representation in Brussels.
2. ECU stood for European Currency Unit. This was an artificial unit of account in which all common Community charges and payments were nominated. It was made up of a basket of all Community currencies and initially was roughly equivalent to US$1. It was superseded by the euro from 1999.

## Chapter 11

1. *GATT Activities 1993*, GATT, Geneva, 1994, p. 24.

## Chapter 12

1. Dr David Hallam and Professor the Lord Peston, *The Political Economy of Europe's Banana Trade*, Department of Agricultural and Food Economics, University of Reading, January 1997, p. 44.
2. Chiquita Petition to the Section 301 Committee, Office of the US Trade Representative, September 1994.
3. See Chapter 9 for details of the regime.
4. Chiquita Petition to the Section 301 Committee.
5. Roy Jenkins, *Churchill*, Macmillan, London, 2001, p. 665.
6. Providing duty-free entry for most products grown or manufactured in the Caribbean states.
7. Comments of the Dole Food Company, Inc., submitted to the US Trade Representative, 16 May 1996.
8. For example, *Time*, 31 March 1997 and 7 February 2000. The very forthright comments in the latter are quoted in Chapter 15.
9. *Time*, 31 March 1997.

## Chapter 13

1. There were four reports, one for Guatemala and Honduras jointly, since they had filed a joint submission, and one each in response to each of the other complainants. Much of each report was identical.

## Chapter 14

1. *Time* magazine, 7 February 2000.
2. HR 2106, the Small Business Trade Protection Act.

## Chapter 15

1. Brent Borrell, 'Beyond EU Bananarama 1993: The Story Gets Worse', Centre for International Economics, Canberra, June 1996, Abstract.
2. The various critiques are summarised in Dr David Hallam and Professor the Lord Peston, *The Political Economy of Europe's Banana Trade*, Department of Agricultural and Food Economics, University of Reading, January 1997, ch. 3.
3. Prof. J.P. McInerney, 'An Economic Commentary on the Latin American Submissions to the GATT', October 1993, privately circulated.
4. *Financial Times*, 20 January 1995.
5. Brent Borrell and Maw-Cheng Yang, 'EC Bananarama 1992', Policy Research Working Paper, International Economics Department, World Bank, 1992.
6. Ibid.

## Chapter 16

1. *Wall Street Journal*, 15 December 1999.
2. The Commission would do this through the Banana Management Committee. This is an essentially advisory body on which all member states are represented. It cannot block a Commission proposal. But if they muster a qualified majority vote *against* the Commission proposal, the Council can overrule it within a limited time span (normally one month).
3. *Wall Street Journal* Europe, 17 April 2001.

## Chapter 17

1. Seventy-three ACP countries had signed the Agreement by 23 June 2000. There were 79 in 2003. Accession is open to any independent state with comparable economic and social structures.

## Chapter 18

1. FAO Banana Statistics CCP; BA/TF01/2 Presented at the Intergovernmental Group on Bananas and Tropical Fruits, San José, Costa Rica 4–8 December 2001.
2. Euro PA & Associates, Commentary and Analysis of Bananarama III, prepared for the Caribbean Banana Exporters Association, February 1995.
3. Arthur D. Little, 'Study of the Impact of the Banana CMO on the Banana Industry in the European Union, Summary, 1995', presented at a seminar in Brussels.
4. Peter Clegg, *The Caribbean Banana Trade from Colonialism to Globalization*, Palgrove, London, 2002.
5. *Banana Exports from the Caribbean since 1992*, study by National Economic Research Associates (NERA), Economic Consultants, 2003, Section 2.7. This is a trade estimate. Customs & Excise give a figure of 781,000 tonnes and Eurostat 833,000, but these both include re-exports to other member states.
6. European Commission Response to Special Report No 7/2002 of the European Court of Auditors on the sound financial management of the common organisation of the markets in the banana sector, para. 84.
7. *Banana Exports from the Caribbean since 1992*, table 4.4. In 1992, Wibdeco had given a figure of 27,000 to the House of Commons Agriculture Committee, but this was subsequently considered an over-estimate.
8. FAO Intergovernmental Group on Bananas, December 2001.

## Chapter 19

1. Resolution of the ACP Council of Ministers meeting in the Dominican Republic, 25–27 June 2002. Addressed to the Council, Parliament and Commission of the European Union.
2. *Banana Trade News Bulletin*, 28 July 2003, published by Banana Link, Norwich.
3. Ibid.
4. *Banana Exports from the Caribbean since 1992*, study by National Economic Research Associates (NERA), Economic Consultants, London, 2003, table 4.10.
5. 'Sainsbury Puts Consumer First', *Fresh Produce Journal*, Supplement, July 2003.
6. *A Valuable Commodity: The UK Banana Business at a Crossroads*, the Banana Group in association with the Centre for Economics and Business Research, 1996, published by Beechey Morgan Associates.
7. 'A War Without Winners', *Fresh Produce Journal*, Supplement, July 1993.
8. Editorial, *Fresh Produce Journal*, July 2003, Supplement.
9. *Race to the Bottom: Banana Workers' Rights in Ecuador*, published by Banana

Link in collaboration with War on Want, with funding from the UK Department for International Development, p. 5.
10. Ibid., p. 15. Incident at Alamo, 5 May 2002.
11. Ibid., p. 5, quoting an interview with the *Financial Times* in 2000.
12. 'Work in Progress', Presentation to the Banana Management Committee of the European Commission, 27 June 2003.
13. See Chapter 9, p. 62.

## Chapter 20

1. Axel Klein, 'The Ganja Industry and Alternative Development in St Vincent', unpublished, Drugscope 2003.
2. Ibid., pp. 6, 8, 17.

## Chapter 21

1. FAO Intergovernmental Group on Bananas, December 2001.
2. Caribbean Organics and Fair Trade Conference, Lancaster House, London, 21 March 2002.
3. Ian Bretman, Deputy Director, Fair Trade Foundation, London, quoted in *Fresh Produce Journal*, Supplement, July 2003.
4. Ibid.
5. Caribbean Organics and Fair Trade Conference.

## Chapter 22

1. 'The World Trade Organisation: The EU Mandate after Seattle', House of Lords Select Committee on the European Union, 10th Report, p. 87. Supplementary evidence from Mr Phillip Lee.
2. From an address given at the Fort Young Hotel, Roseau, 11 September 1997.
3. House of Lords Select Committee on the European Union, 10th Report, Memorandum of Evidence submitted by Dr Peter Holmes and Professor Jim Rollo.
4. House of Commons International Development Committee, Session 1997–98, Fourth Report, Renegotiation of the Lomé Convention, vol. 1, para. 138.
5. Report of Chairman, WTO Agriculture Committee, 7 July 2003.
6. 'A Study of Alternative Special and Differential Arrangements for Small Economies', prepared for the Commonwealth Secretariat by Michael Davenport.
7. WTO Secretariat, *Trade and Economic Performance: The Role of Economic Size*, WT/COMTD/SE/W/5, http://docsonline.wto.org/gen_search.asp.

# Appendix

1. Paragraph 84 of the Commission Reply, to Special Report No 7/2002 of the European Court of Auditors on the sound financial management of the common organisation of the markets in the banana sector.

# Index

A quota, 116, 122
Adenauer, Konrad, 38
Africa Growth and Opportunity
    Act, USA, 99
African Caribbean and Pacific
    countries (ACP), 4, 53,
    55–6, 59–62, 66–7, 71–4, 76,
    83–4, 86, 88–9, 93–4, 96, 97,
    113–17, 120, 122, 130, 141, 161,
    167; African producers, 69;
    banana exports, 143; banana
    producers, 54, 80, 88, 137, 144;
    country allocation dismantled,
    132; direct aid proposals,
    101–3; EU commitments (Lomé
    Convention), 41, 91, 111, 121,
    145; income support proposal,
    63; market share, 129; needs,
    169; products, 87; quota, 112,
    116, 118–19, 123; single quota,
    148; tariff exemption, 104; tariff
    preference, 68, 79; volume limit,
    58
American Finance Corporation
    (AFC), 44
AMK Sealed Caps, 44
Andean Trade Preference Act,
    81
Antilles Products, 18–19
Asda, supermarket chain, 139
Asia: banana evolution, 5; demand,
    50; market, 75
Austria, 92–3

B licence system, 68, 76, 80, 92, 96,
    128, 147, 170
B quota, 59–60, 73, 88, 116, 122, 167
banana: Asian evolution, 5; Black
    Sigatoka disease, 132; carton
    boxing, 29, 48–9; Cavendish
    variety, 48; Fair Trade, 157; Gros
    Michel variety, 29, 48; Lacatan
    variety, 29; organic, 134, 147,
    155–7; Panama disease (fusarial
    wilt), 48; price collapse, 138;
    production figures, 19; structural
    surplus, 154; world trade figures,
    75
'banana fatigue', 142
Banana Framework Agreement
    (BFA), 71–2, 74, 77, 80–81, 83–5,
    109, 130, 132, 134–5, 169
Banana Link, 47
Banana Protocol: Contonou, 121,
    142; Lomé Convention, 41
'Banana War', 23
'Bananarama' reports, 101–2
Bananera Naboa, 46
Barbados, 152
Barchefsky, Charlene, 78, 117–18
Barclays Bank, 132
Belgium, 37–8, 60–61
Belize, 27, 34, 54, 57, 74, 78, 129;
    Big Creek port, 149; EU exports,
    148; privatisation, 132
Black, Eli, 44
Borrell, Brent, 101–4

Boston Fruit Company (United Fruit), 6
Brazil, 23; banana production levels, 42; brazil nut deal, 66
British Cameroons, 18, 23
British Honduras, 132
Brittan, Leon, 54, 118
Bush, George H., 70, 81

C quota, 115, 116, 118
Cameroon, 16, 39, 42, 49, 74, 145; export increase, 133; investment, 147
Canada, 16, 99; banana market, 14; Jamaican bananas, 15
Canadian Banana Company (United Fruit), 18
Canary Islands, 5, 8, 23, 40, 133
Caribbean, the, 1; banana appearance, 25; banana farms, 2, 146; banana identity need, 158; banana industry, 11, 107; Basin Initiative, 81; geo-political insignificance, 79; governments, 77, 101
Caribbean Banana Exporters Association, 54, 148
Caribbean Economic Community (CARICOM), 35, 78
'Caribbean Proposal', 114
Cavendish banana variety, 48
Central America, 6
Centre for Economic Studies, Canberra, 101
Chamberlain, Joseph, 5, 7–8, 11, 14
Chamberlain, Neville, 14
Charles, Dame Eugenia, 35, 53–4
Chiquita (ex-United Fruit), 6, 43–6, 48–9, 51, 53, 57, 77–8, 80, 92, 108, 111, 113, 118, 133, 135, 169; Europe losses, 76; International Division, 141; market share, 127; political donations, 82; political influence, 81–2, 99, 109–10, 128; worker exploitation, 75; world trade share, 75

Chris International Foods, 30–31
Churchill, Winston, 79
CIA, Guatemala invasion, 43
*Cincinnati Enquirer*, case, 109–10
Clinton, Bill: administration, 70, 78–9, 82
Cold War: end of, 108; post-, 79
Colombia, 15, 42, 51, 66, 71–2, 75, 80, 81, 85, 93, 134; EU exports, 135; Fair Trade bananas, 155; plantations, 6; wage levels, 46
Commonwealth, the: banana tariff protection, 23; Development Corporation, 33, 132; Secretariat, 164; Sugar Agreement, 3, 22
comparative advantage, theory of, 105
Compton, John, 146
Cotonou Fiji: 'Partnership Agreement' (Lomé), 120–23, 142–4, 165, 171
Costa Rica, 6, 15, 42, 48, 66, 71–2, 75, 80–81, 85, 93, 129, 134; EU exports, 135; Fair Trade bananas, 155
Council of Ministers, EC/EU, 53, 57, 92–3, 112, 116, 137
Cuba, 6, 28

De Gaulle, Charles, 37
deficiency payments system, 63, 104–5, 108, 117, 131, 145
Del Monte, 43–4, 46, 51, 82, 128, 133, 139
Delors, Jacques, 56
Denmark, 60–62, 64, 92, 94, 98; EC accession, 37
Denning, Lord, 25
diversification, 143
Doha Round, WTO, 161, 164, 166; Conference, 122
Dole Food Company (ex Standard Fruit), 43, 46, 49, 51, 75, 78, 118, 128, 133; market share, 127
Dole, Robert, 81
dollar bananas, 26, 55, 59, 73, 102, 122, 126, 128; illegal imports,

130–31, 138; 'quota', 62, 93, 114, 138; UK, 30
dollar, US: EC/$ exchange rate, 35; sterling rate, 11; UK shortage, 3
Dominica, 2, 16, 18, 20–21, 35, 53, 63, 114, 143, 159
Dominican Republic, 25, 74, 133, 147, 155–7; Fair Trade bananas, 155
drought, 21, 131; Jamaica, 24
drug trafficking, 107, 150
Dunkel, Arthur, 55

Eastern Caribbean currency, 35
Eastern Europe, 114; demand, 50, 75
East Germany, banana consumption economies of scale, 48, 133
Ecuador, 26, 42–3, 72–3, 85, 93–7, 99, 111, 113, 118, 122, 144, 157, 162; exports, 134–6; export retaliation, 32; Fair trade bananas, 155; plantation ownership, 45; US WTO backing, 83; wage levels, 46, 141
El Niño, 45
Elder, Dempster & Co, 5, 7, 9
Elders & Fyffes Ltd, 8–9, 11, 45
environment, protection, 47
Esquivel, Manuel, 78
ethical prices, 158
Europe: banana growers of, 38, 62–3, 73, 87–8, 92–3, 131, 169; sugar beet industry, 20
European Economic Community (EEC): British accession, 4, 25, 36, 39; original members, 37 European Community/ European Union (EC/EU), 49–50, 72, 80–81, 83–4, 89, 101, 118, 120, 123–4, 141, 160; -ACP Convention commitments (Lomé), 40, 73, 79, 88, 103–4, 158, 169; ACP trade, 128; access preferences, 2; agricultural support prices, 58; banana regime, 55, 71, 74, 76–7, 104, 125, 127; British role, 3; Commission, 55–6, 59, 62, 71, 94, 111–12,

114–16, 130, 132, 138, 142–4, 148, 151, 162, 167, 171; Community Development staff, 152; Council of Ministers (see Council of Ministers); Ecuador imports, 134; enlarged, 145; Jamaica aid, 149; legislation process, 91; licensing procedures, 87; protection of domestic growers (see Europe); single market regime, 44, 50, 67; Special Framework of Assistance, 147; –USA banana stand-off, 1, 4; –US banana agreement 2001, 137, 142, 144, 152; –US trade sanctions against, 78, 95–9, 109, 161; voting packages, 64; world import share, 42
European Court of Justice, 44, 62, 112
European Parliament, 38, 53, 91, 115, 137

Fair Trade: bananas, 157–8; Labelling Organisation International, 155; movement, 154–5, 166
Finland, 92–3
first come, first served system (FCFS), 113–19
First World War, UK debt, 11
France, 18, 37, 66, 92, 142; banana policy, 63; Caribbean Islands, 40; restrictive import regime, 38–9
free-trade ideology, 102, 105, 144
French Cameroons, 23
Fruit Importers of Ireland (FII), 45
Fyffe, Edward Wathen, 5
Fyffes, 24, 27, 30, 44–5, 54, 129, 132, 148; market share, 128; UK dominance, 19

Geest, John van, 19
Geest Industries Ltd, 19, 24, 30, 54, 76; market share, 128–9
General Agreement on Trade in Services (GATS), 71, 83, 87; principle of, 88

General Agreement on Tariffs and
Trade (GATT), 23, 26, 56–7, 66,
89–90, 108; Article I, 68; Article
III.4, 68; Article XIII, 65, 85–6,
88, 96–7, 112, 160; Article XIII.4,
87; Article XXV, 160; Article
XXV.5, 69, 84; Article XXVIII,
66, 68, 144; Generalised
System of Preferences, 81,
159; 'Grandfather clause', 67;
Latin America complaints, 77;
membership, 85; 1993 case, 61;
non-discrimination principle,
65; Protocols of Provisonal
Accession, 67; rules, 71; Uruguay
Round, 55, 70, 159, 168; US
complaint, 32; waivers, 83
Germany, 37–8, 55, 58, 61–2, 91–4,
125, 133; duty-free bananas, 57;
Fair Trade market share, 156;
organic banana market, 157;
retail prices, 126
Ghana, 74; Fair Trade bananas, 155
Gold Standard, UK abandonment,
14
Gordon, Bishop, 7
Greece: Cretan banana production,
39–40; EC accession, 37
Grenada, 18, 156
Gros Michel banana variety, 29, 48
Guadeloupe, 39, 63
Guatemala, 42, 44, 71, 83–4, 122,
132; CIA invasion, 43; land
reform, 43
Gummer, John Selwyn, 35, 53, 57,
60, 61

Hawaii Banana Industry
Association, 77
Heath, Edward, 37
historic-based system, EU–USA
agreement, 118
Hodgson, Mr Justice, 30–31
Hoggarth, Marcus, 140
Honduras, 15–16, 42, 48, 75, 83, 122;
plantations, 6; wage levels, 46
House of Commons, UK:

Agriculture Committee, 35;
International Development
Committee, 163; Select
Committee Report, 1993, 146
Hudson, James, 5
hurricanes, 21, 129, 151; Allen 1980,
27, 33; David 1979, 27; Jamaica
1903, 9; 'licences', 87–8; 1932–3,
13; 1944, 22

Imperial preference: idea of, 7
introduction, 14
import duties, 65–6
import licences, 76, 92
India, production levels, 42
intellectual property rights, 71
International Labour Organisation,
166
International Narcotics Control
Strategy Report, 107
International Sugar Agreement, 167
Irish Republic, 38, 45; EC accession,
37; Windwards bananas, 18
irrigation, 34, 150, 152–3
Italy, 37, 66, 142; restrictive import
regime, 38–9
Ivory coast, 39, 42, 49, 74, 145;
export increase, 133; investment,
147; UK market access, 24

Jamaica, 5, 8, 11, 23, 39, 49, 54,
56–7, 107, 114, 129, 132, 134,
140; Banana Board, 24–7;
Banana Co-operative Marketing
Association, 14; Banana Export
Company (BECO), 33; Banana
Producers Association, 12, 16–17,
19, 54, 148; British involvement,
10; Co-operative Marketing
Association Law 19, 13; estate
closure, 131; farm concentration,
21, 33–4, 149; grower prices, 15;
hurricanes, 9, 22; production
costs, 145; production levels,
28; quality standards, 32; UK
market, 7, 18; US market, 6
James, Edison, 159, 172

Japan, 89, 99
Jenkins, Roy, 79
Jones, Alfred, 7–9

Kantor, Mickey, 80, 109
Keith, Minor, 6
Korea, access to, 50

labelling, 48
Lacatan, banana variety, 29
Lamy, Pascal, 117
Latin America, 9, 20–21, 35, 39–40,
42, 53, 55, 63, 74, 134, 141,
146, 154; banana trade, 1, 66,
105; carton boxing, 29, 48–9;
Chiquita land control, 75; export
volumes, 50; GATT complaint,
77; grower prices, 15; planation
ownership, 45, 48; plantation
size, 2, 34, 49; US backing, 71;
worker exploitation, 46–7
Latin American Workers Union Co-
ordination (COLSIB), 46
limes, 20
Lindner, Carl, 44, 81, 109; political
donations, 82; political influence,
169
Liverpool, 5
Lomé, 96, 143
Lomé Convention, 40, 45, 60,
67, 73, 84–5, 88, 92, 96, 104,
114, 143; Article 168, 87;
commitments, 79; First, 41;
Fourth, 142, 170; Fourth expiry,
120, 121; Protocol 5, 86
Luxembourg, 37–8; dairy industry, 64

Maharaj, Krishna, 31
Major, John, 56
Manley, Michael, 28, 56
marijuana/ganja, 107, 150–51
Marrakesh meeting, Uruguay
Round, 71, 77; Agreement, 71
Martinique, 39, 63
Mexico, 83, 132
Miami, US–Caribbean Summit
1994, 78

Morrisons, supermarket chain, 139
most-favoured nation status, 65, 71

Navigation Acts, 3
'negative tariff', 108, 165
Netherlands, 37, 55, 61, 94; Fair
Trade market share, 155–6
New Zealand, butter, 64
Nicaragua, 66, 71–2, 85, 134, 141;
wage levels, 46
Nigeria, 23

Office of the US Trade
Representative (USTR), 77–8,
80–81, 97–9, 108–9, 114, 128
oil, 1973 price shock, 28

Panama, 42, 48, 75, 122, 135; Canal,
136; plantations, 6; wage levels,
46
Peru, 45
Philippines, 50; banana production,
42
Portugal, 61, 64
Portugal, domestic producer
protection Madeira, 39–40; EC
accession, 37
producer organisations, 12

regional free-trade areas, 120;
agreements, 142, 165
retail prices, 130–31, 139;
comparative, 126
Robinson, Randall, 106
Roosevelt, Franklin D., 79
rum: Caribbean, 3; protection, 41

St Lucia, 2, 16, 18, 57, 63, 146; US
base, 21
St Vincent and the Grenadines, 2,
18, 152; marijuana/ganja, 107,
150–51
Sainsbury, supermarket chain,
139–40, 156
Santo Domingo, plantations, 6
scarring, 29
Scotland, cashmere products, 98

Seattle, protests, 160
Second World War, 15; Jamaica, 16
Sheehan, John, 107
shipping, 12, 103, 106, 116; advance
    planning, 73, 113; boxes, 29;
    costs, 21, 34, 43, 150; distances,
    136, 148; wartime lack, 16;
    Windward Islands service, 143,
    157
Single European Act 1986, 37–8
small vulnerable economies (SVEs),
    163–4, 172
Somalia, 39
Spain, 66; Canary Islands
    production protection, 39–40;
    consumer loyalty, 133; EC
    accession, 37
'special export certificates', 73
Standard Fruit (Dole), 14, 44, 48
sterling area, 11, 18
Stockley, Arthur J., 7–9, 13
strike price auction system, 112, 113
sugar, 20, 22; cane, 19; plantations,
    150; protectionism, 41, 167; UK
    beet, 3
supermarkets, 158; competition, 133;
    price power, 4, 139–41, 166
Surinam, 27, 34, 54, 129, 148; strike,
    140; Surland company, 131
Sutherland, Peter, 70
Sweden, 91–4
Switzerland, Fair Trade market
    share, 155

tariffs: future levels, 66, 122, 124,
    154; in-quota, 67–8, 72; -only
    regime, 115, 149, 171; out-of-
    quota, 68; preferences, 86; quota
    system, 56–8, 60, 68, 72, 74, 80,
    84, 86–7, 93, 104–5, 108, 111,
    116–17, 125, 136–8, 144, 165, 169;
    'tariffication', 55–7, 168
technology transfer, 149
Tesco, supermarket chain, 139
Thatcher, Margaret, government,
    32, 37
tourism, 105–6, 143, 150

trade unions: democratic, 155;
    intimidation of, 47, 141
Transafrica group, 106
Treaty of Rome 1958, 37–8, 50, 62,
    125; Amsterdam amendment, 163
Tripartite Agreement 1936, 13

United Brands (ex-United fruit),
    33–4
United Fruit Company (Chiquita),
    6, 8–9, 11–14, 18, 25, 33, 43–5, 48
United Nations: Food and
    Agriculture Organisation (FAO),
    48; Trustee Committee, 23
United Kingdom (UK), 66, 92,
    117, 142, 143; banana history, 5;
    banana import regimes, 14, 21,
    26, 30–31, 33, 38, 44, 66, 168;
    Brazilian bananas, 23; Canary
    Island imports, 40; Caribbean
    commitment, 2–3, 8; Department
    of Trade, 32; EC/EU Presidency,
    53, 60, 68, 91, 93; EEC accession,
    4, 25, 36, 39, 104; ethical trade
    policy, 35; Fair Trade bananas,
    155–6; Fyffes dominance,
    19; House of Commons, 35,
    146, 163; Imperial Economic
    Committee, 11–13; Import Duties
    Bill 1932, 15; Iraq air patrols, 98;
    Jamaica banana involvement,
    6–7, 10; Ministry of Agriculture,
    Fisheries and Food (MAFF),
    27, 146; Ministry of Food, 15,
    18; organic banana market,
    157; Overseas Development
    Administration (Department for
    International Development), 63;
    Restrictive Trade Practices Acts,
    24; retail prices, 126–7, 133; sugar
    beet, 22; supermarkets, 139–40,
    154; wartime diet, 16; West Indies
    Royal Commission 1938–9, 20,
    34
UK/Jamaica Banana Quality
    monitoring Group, 32
United States of America (USA), 2,

11, 26, 57, 63, 71, 74, 84, 89, 94, 100, 111, 115–17, 135, 144–5, 170; anti-trust actions, 43–4; banana market, 14; Caribbean policy shift, 108; –Caribbean summit 1994, 78; Chapter 11 protection, 118; commercial interests, 79; Company tax breaks, 162; Congressional Black Caucus, 106; –EU agreement, 137, 142, 144, 152; –EU stand-off, 1, 4, 107; Farm Bureau, 108; 'fast-track' power, 70; GATT complaint 1972, 32; Jamaica bananas, 6; protective barriers, 165; Republican Party, 82; St Lucia base, 21; sugar protectionism, 167; 'tariffication' preference, 168; trade legislation, 91, 99, 127; Trade Representative, USTR (see Office of); trade sanctions use, 95–9, 109, 161; West Coast imports, 136; world import share, 42; WTO complaint, 83; WTO power, 160
University of Exeter, 102
Uruguay Round, GATT, 55, 69–70, 84, 159, 168

Vaccaro Brothers Company (Standard Fruit), 43
vanilla, 20
Venezuela, 66, 71–2, 85, 134
volume quota, 57

wage levels, pressure on, 141
Wal-Mart, 139
Waters, Maxine, 106–7
West Africa, 148; banana industry,

26, 169; francophone, 133
Wilson, Harold, 64
Windward Islands, 12, 16, 18–19, 23–6, 33, 39, 49, 54, 76, 89–90, 107, 114, 129, 133, 143, 149, 164–5, 171–2; banana price collapse, 138, 140; economic vulnerability, 163; Fair Trade bananas, 155; farming structure, 20–21, 34; growers, 131, 150; labour laws, 158; legal advisers WTO exclusion, 161; oil price impact, 28; production costs, 145, 150; Production Recovery Programme, 152; rationalisation need, 153; shipping service, 103, 106; tourism, 105; trading bodies, 27; Wibdeco, 129, 148, 151
World Bank, 27, 102, 164
World Trade Organisation (WTO), 1–2, 55, 65, 69–70, 72, 80, 84, 89, 93, 95–6, 109, 111, 115, 120, 128, 130, 162, 172; battles with, 170–71; Dispute Settlement Board, 94; Disputes Settlement Procedure, 83, 91, 168; Disputes Settlement Understanding (DSU), 159; first banana case 1999, 108, 132, 143–5; Geneva HQ, 165; inflexibility, 166; panel, 99; procedures, 100, 164; representation exclusion, 160–61; rules, 97, 112, 142; second case 2001, 123–5, 137, 147, 151–2; waiver, 118–19, 122

Zoellick, Robert, 117

*Zed Books titles of related interest*

Stolen Fruit: The Tropical Commodities Disaster
*Peter Robbins*
Hb ISBN 1 84277 280 5   £32.95 $55.00
Pb ISBN 1 84277 281 3   £9.99 $17.50

Behind the Scenes at the WTO: The Real World of International
Trade Negotiations/Lessons of Cancun – UPDATED EDITION
*Fatoumata Jawara and Aileen Kwa*
Hb ISBN 1 84277 532 4   £36.95 $19.95
Pb ISBN 1 84277 533 2   £12.99 $59.95

Reclaiming Development: An Alternative Economic Policy Manual
*Ha-Joon Chang and Ilene Grabel*
Hb ISBN 1 84277 200 7   £32.95 $55.00
Pb ISBN 1 84277 201 5   £9.99 $17.50

Free Trade: Myth, Reality and Alternatives
*Graham Dunkley*
Hb ISBN 1 85649 862 x   £32.95 $55.00
Pb ISBN 1 85649 863 8   £9.99 $17.50

The Economist's Tale: A Consultant Encounters Hunger
and the World Bank
*Peter Griffiths*
Hb ISBN 1 84277 184 1   £49.95 $69.95
Pb ISBN 1 84277 185 x   £15.95 $25.00

Caribbean Drugs: From Criminalization to Harm Reduction
*Edited by Axel Klein, Marcus Day and Anthony Harriott*
Published in association with Drugscope
Hb ISBN 1 84277 498 0   £49.95 $75.00
Pb ISBN 1 84277 499 9   £16.95 $25.00

A People's World: Alternatives to Economic Globalization
*John Madeley*
Hb ISBN 1 84277 222 8   £32.95 $55.00
Pb ISBN 1 84277 223 6   £ 9.99 $17.50

Who Owes Who? 50 Questions about World Debt
*Damien Millet and Eric Toussaint*
Hb ISBN 1 84277 426 3   £36.95 $65.00
Pb ISBN 1 84277 427 1   £12.99 $19.95

Unholy Trinity: The IMF, World Bank and WTO
*Richard Peet*
Hb ISBN 1 84277 072 1   £49.95 $69.95
Pb ISBN 1 84277 073 X   £15.95 $25.00

Fat Cats and Running Dogs: The Enron Stage of Capitalism
*Vijay Prashad*
Hb ISBN 1 84277 260 0   £27.95
Pb ISBN 1 84277 261 9   £9.99

The Three Waves of Globalization: A History of a Developing
Global Consciousness
*Robbie Robertson*
Hb ISBN 1 85649 860 3   £49.95 $75.00
Pb ISBN 1 85649 861 1   £12.99 $25.00

100 Ways of Seeing an Unequal World
*Bob Sutcliffe*
Hb ISBN 1 85649 813 1   £49.95 $69.95
Pb ISBN 1 85649 814 X   £15.95 $25.00

For full details of these titles and Zed's general and subject catalogues, please write to: The Marketing Department, Zed Books, 7 Cynthia Street, London N1 9JF, UK or email Sales@zedbooks.demon.co.uk

Visit our website at: http://www.zedbooks.co.uk